World War I
The Home Front

Teachers Guide

A Supplemental Teaching Unit
from the Records of the National Archives

**SCHOOL OF EDUCATION
CURRICULUM LABORATORY
UM-DEARBORN**

NATIONAL
ARCHIVES

National Archives Trust Fund Board
National Archives and Records Administration

A B C ⬥ C L I O

ABC – CLIO, Inc
130 Cremona Drive, P.O. Box 1911
Santa Barbara, CA 93116-1911
ISBN 1-57607-784-5

U. S. DEPARTMENT OF LABOR
W. B. WILSON, SECRETARY

Issued through
INFORMATION AND EDUCATION SERVICE
Roger W. Babson, Chief

CL
940.3
c.1

Other Units in this Series:

The Constitution: Evolution of a Government

The Bill of Rights: Evolution of Personal Liberties

The United States Expands West: 1785-1842

WOMAN IN INDUSTRY SERVICE
Westward Expansion: 1842-1912

The Civil War: Soldiers and Civilians

This contains a copy of the statement of principles concerning the employment of
women in war work as adopted by the War Labor Policies Board. It defines what kind
The Progressive Years: 1898-1917
of work women may perform, how they shall best be introduced, under what conditions
they should be employed and what work should be prohibited.
The 1920's

Employers should avail themselves of the assistance of the Woman in Industry Service
The Great Depression and The New Deal
for advice on the best methods of introducing women and the working conditions which
should be established.
World War II: The Home Front

STANDARDS FOR THE EMPLOYMENT OF WOMEN OUTLINED BY THE WAR
The United States At War: 1944
LABOR POLICIES BOARD
The Truman Years: 1945-1953

The War Labor Policies Board, for the Department of Labor, announces the Govern-
Peace and Prosperity: 1953-1961
ment's attitude toward the employment of women in war industry. The principles set
forth will underlie the work of the Woman in Industry Service, of which Miss Mary Van
Kleeck has been appointed Director and Miss Mary Anderson, Assistant Director.

The existing shortage of labor, aggravated daily by the military and naval demands
of the Government which requires a greatly increased production of war materials and at
the same time the withdrawal from civil occupations of about a quarter of a million additional recruits each month, necessitates widespread recourse to the labor of women in the
United States.

In order that their services may be fully utilized and their working power conserved,
a clearly defined policy is needed which shall determine what kinds of work women should
perform, how they should best be introduced, under what conditions they should be employed, and what work should be prohibited.

Standards as to hours, night work, wages, and conditions of labor have already been
defined by the Government in orders issued by the Chief of Ordnance and the Quartermaster General, and in the recommendations made by the War Labor Board, which should
be observed by all employers.

First. The shortage of labor in essential war industries should be met in part by
further introducing women into occupations easily filled by them, such as clerical and
cashier service and accounting in manufacturing, mercantile and financial establishments
and in the offices of transportation companies and other public utilities; such as sales

Table of Contents

Foreword

The National Archives and Records Service is responsible for the preservation and use of the permanently valuable records of the federal government. These materials provide evidence of the activities of the government from 1774 to the present in the form of written and printed documents, maps and posters, sound recordings, photographs, films, and computer tapes. These rich archival sources are useful to all: federal officials seeking information on past government activities, citizens needing data for use in legal matters, historians interpreting the past, journalists researching stories, students preparing term papers, and persons tracing their ancestry or satisfying their curiosity about particular historical events. The National Archives serves as the nation's memory for a multitude of purposes.

As part of the continuing effort to make these records available to the public in forms most appropriate to its needs, our Office of Educational Programs began in 1970 a program designed to introduce these vast resources to secondary school students. School classes visiting the Archives were given the opportunity to work with archival materials as historians use them. Staff members developed activities to engage students in examining and interpreting original sources; teachers and students responded enthusiastically. As a result of this success, the National Archives devised a plan to reach larger numbers of students across the nation by publishing a series of supplementary teaching units from National Archives sources. This particular unit, *World War I: The Home Front*, is the first in the series. We hope that these materials will bring you and your students closer to the pleasures and the perils of working with primary sources and will enhance your classroom program.

JAMES B. RHOADS
Archivist of the United States
1979

...to bring you and your students the excitement and satisfaction of working with primary sources and to enhance your instructional program.

Preface

- This unit is made up of 5 exercises.

- Each exercise includes reproductions of documents from the National Archives and suggests classroom activities based on these documents.

World War I: The Home Front is a teaching unit designed to supplement and enliven your students' study of World War I by engaging them in the process by which history is written. The unit is made up of five exercises that relate to life on the home front. Each exercise uses reproductions of documents from the National Archives and suggests classroom activities based on these documents. The documents include letters, photographs, petitions, posters, and other documents. Students practice the historian's skills as they complete exercises using these documents to gather information, identify points of view, evaluate evidence, form hypotheses, and draw conclusions. If you wish to do all of the exercises in the unit, schedule about two weeks of class time.

The documents in this unit do not reflect every topic usually included in a history or government textbook. In some instances, the federal government had no interest in or authority over a given event and therefore created no records on it. In other cases, documents in the National Archives on several historic topics proved to be difficult to use in the classroom due to problems of legibility, length, or format.

National Archives education specialists Mary Alexander and CeCe Byers and Academic and Curricular Programs Director Elsie Freeman Finch developed this publication. We are pleased to issue a revised and updated set of these documentary teaching materials.

WYNELL B. SCHAMEL
LEE ANN POTTER
Education Specialists
2001

> ***World War I: The Home Front*** is a teaching unit designed to supplement and enliven your students' study of World War I by engaging them in the process by which history is written.

$\mathscr{A}$cknowledgments

Many people helped in the original production of this unit. They included National Archives staff members Joseph Howerton, Donald Mosholder, Layne Moore, and George Perros.

Special thanks go to Virginia Cardwell Purdy, formerly Director of the Education Division, Office of Educational Programs, National Archives and Records Service, whose imagination sparked the project. The advice, criticism, and encouragement of Charles L. Mitsakos, Andover, MA, Public Schools, were invaluable during the development stages.

Others here and across the country whose stern criticism moved the project along included Shelby Bale, Richard Bennett, Edith James, Irving Morrissett, Nancy Malan, Geraldine H. Rosenthal, Viki Sand, J. Samuel Walker, and Thomas Weinland. Lois Himmel, a graduate intern in this office at the time, researched and developed the annotated bibliography.

During the republication process, we were ably assisted by George Mason University intern Adam Jevec; volunteers, Elizabeth S. Lourie, Jane Douma Pearson, and Donald Alderson; and National Archives staff members Michael Hussey, A.J. Daverede, Patrick Osborn, Amy Patterson, Kate Flaherty, Donald Roe, and Charles Mayn.

$\mathcal{P}$ublisher's Note

$\mathbf{P}$rimary source documents have long been a cornerstone of ABC-CLIO's commitment to producing high-quality, learner-centered history and social studies resources. When our nation's students have the opportunity to interact with the undiluted artifacts of the past, they can better understand the breadth of the human experience and the present state of affairs.

It is with great enthusiasm that we celebrate the release of this series of teaching units designed in partnership with the National Archives—materials that we hope will bring historical context and deeper knowledge to U.S. middle and high school students. Each unit has been revised and updated, including new bibliographic references. Each teaching unit has been correlated to the curriculum standards for the teaching of social studies and history developed by the National Council for the Social Studies and the National Center for History in the Schools.

For more effective use of these teaching units in the classroom, each booklet is accompanied by an interactive CD-ROM which includes exercise worksheets, digital images of original documents, and, for four titles, sound recordings. A videocassette of motion pictures accompanies the teaching unit *The United States At War: 1944*. For those who would like to order facsimiles of primary source documents in their original sizes, or additional titles in this series, we have included an order form to make it easy for you to do so.

The mission of the National Archives is "to ensure ready access to the essential evidence that documents the rights of American citizens, the actions of Federal officials, and the national experience."

These units go a long way toward fulfilling that mission, helping the next generation of American citizens develop a clear understanding of the nation's past and a firm grasp of the role of the individual in guiding the nation's future. ABC-CLIO is honored to be part of this process.

BECKY SNYDER
Publisher & Vice President
ABC-CLIO Schools

$\mathbf{T}$he mission of the National Archives is "to ensure ready access to the essential evidence that documents the rights of American citizens, the actions of Federal officials, and the national experience."

Teaching With Documents Curriculum Standards Correlations

The National Council for the Social Studies and the National Center for History in the Schools have developed a set of comprehensive curriculum standards for the teaching of social studies and history. Take a look at how thoroughly the Teaching With Documents series supports the curriculum.

	The Constitution: Evolution of a Government	The Bill of Rights: Evolution of Personal Liberties	The United States Expands West: 1785–1842	Westward Expansion: 1842–1912	The Civil War: Soldiers and Civilians	The Progressive Years: 1898–1917	World War I: The Home Front	The 1920's	The Great Depression and The New Deal World	War II: The Home Front	The United States At War: 1944	The Truman Years: 1945–1953	Peace and Prosperity: 1953–1961
National Council for the Social Studies													
CULTURE—should provide for the study of culture and cultural diversity	•		•	•				•		•			•
TIME, CONTINUITY & CHANGE—should provide for the study of the ways people view themselves in and over time	•	•	•			•	•	•	•	•	•		
PEOPLE, PLACES & ENVIRONMENT—should provide for the study of people, places, and environments	•	•	•	•	•	•		•	•				
INDIVIDUAL DEVELOPMENT & IDENTITY—should provide for the study of individual development and identity	•	•	•	•	•	•	•	•	•				•
INDIVIDUALS, GROUPS & INSTITUTIONS—should provide for the study of interactions among individuals, groups, and institutions	•	•	•	•	•	•		•	•		•	•	•
POWER, AUTHORITY & GOVERNANCE—should provide for the study of how structures of power are created and changed	•	•	•	•	•	•		•	•			•	
PRODUCTION, DISTRIBUTION & CONSUMPTION—should provide for the study of the usage of goods and services	•		•	•	•	•	•	•	•			•	
SCIENCE, TECHNOLOGY & SOCIETY—should provide for the study of relationships among science, technology, and society	•		•	•	•			•			•	•	•
GLOBAL CONNECTIONS—should provide for the study of global connections and interdependence	•		•			•					•	•	•
CIVIC IDEALS & PRACTICES—should provide for the study of the ideals, principles, and practices of citizenship	•	•						•			•		
National Center for History in the Schools													
CHRONOLOGICAL THINKING	•	•	•	•	•	•	•	•	•	•	•	•	•
HISTORICAL COMPREHENSION	•	•	•	•	•	•	•	•	•	•	•	•	•
HISTORICAL ANALYSIS & INTERPRETATION	•	•	•	•	•	•	•	•	•	•	•	•	•
HISTORICAL RESEARCH CAPABILITIES	•	•	•	•	•	•	•	•	•	•	•	•	•
HISTORICAL ISSUES-ANALYSIS & DECISION-MAKING	•	•	•	•	•	•	•	•	•	•	•	•	•

Introduction

This unit contains two elements: 1) a book, which contains a teachers guide and a set of reproductions of print documents, and 2) a CD-ROM, which contains the exercise worksheets from the teachers guide and a set of reproductions of documents in electronic format. In selecting the documents, we applied three standards. First, the documents must be entirely from the holdings of the National Archives and reflect the actions of the federal government or citizens' responses to those actions. Second, most documents must be typical of the hundreds of similar records relating to a particular topic. (Exceptions were made for distinctive or unique documents of compelling historical value.) Third, the documents must be legible and potentially useful for vocabulary development. In selecting documents, we tried to choose those having appeal to young people and their instructors.

Objectives

We have provided an outline of the general objectives for the unit. You will be able to achieve these objectives by completing several, if not all, of the exercises in the unit. Because each exercise aims to develop skills defined in the general objectives, you may be selective and still develop those skills. In addition, each exercise has its own specific objectives.

> **UNIT CONTAINS:**
>
> ◆ **1)** a book, which contains a teachers guide and a set of reproductions of print documents, and
>
> ◆ **2)** a CD-ROM, which contains the exercise worksheets from the teachers guide and a set of reproductions of documents in electronic format.

Outline

This unit on World War I includes five exercises. In choosing topics for the unit, we have sought less to present a balanced range of content than to present topics that offer the maximum potential for developing students' skills. The first topic, "America Moves Toward War," provides a look at public attitudes toward American neutrality in 1917. The second topic, "Women and the War Effort," uses documents to reveal the changing role of women in society. The third, "Uncle Sam Needs You," details government efforts to enlist the support of citizens through print and poster campaigns. The fourth, "Reactions to the Call," focuses on citizen reaction to the government and the war effort. The last topic, "When Johnny Comes Marching Home," examines some of the effects of the conclusion of the war on various elements of American society.

List of Documents

The list of documents gives specific information (e.g., date and name of author) and record group number for each document. Records in the National Archives are arranged in record groups. A typical record group (RG) consists of the records created or accumulated by a department, agency, bureau, or other administrative unit of the federal government. Each record group is identified for retrieval purposes by an arbitrarily assigned record group number; for example, RG 60 (Records of the Department of Justice) or RG 86 (Records of the Women's Bureau). Complete archival citations of all documents are listed in the appendix, p. 48.

Introductory Exercises

Before starting exercises 1-5, it is important to help students become familiar with documents and their importance to the historian who interprets them and writes historical accounts from them. We suggest that you direct students to do the introductory exercises, which can be used with most documents, wherever they are found. The Written Document Analysis, p. 8, is designed to help students analyze systematically any written document in the unit. The Photograph Analysis, p. 9, can be used for the same purpose with any of the photographs in this unit. The Poster Analysis, p. 10, can be used to analyze systematically posters in the unit.

Classroom Exercises

This unit contains five suggested exercises that provide different approaches to the content. These activities incorporate various teaching and learning styles. Like the topics, you may choose among the activities using one or more than one. We encourage you to select those that are most suitable to your needs or to modify the material as it seems appropriate for your class.

Within the explanatory material for each of the five exercises in this unit, you will find the following information:

- ➤ Note to the teacher
- ➤ Classroom time required
- ➤ Objectives (specific)
- ➤ Materials needed
- ➤ Procedures
- ➤ Student worksheets

You may choose to combine several exercises on a topic within the unit. In some instances a document is used in more than one exercise when it is appropriate to the skill or content objectives. We encourage you to select and adapt the exercises and documents that best suit your own teaching style.

Ability Levels

As in our other units, we have developed exercises for students of different abilities. For some topics, we have designed two or more procedures, tailored to different student needs. Throughout the unit we have made an effort to provide exercises in which students use a variety of skills, including reading for understanding; interpreting audiovisual materials, posters, charts, and photographs; and analyzing petitions, resolutions, reports, and correspondence. All lessons have procedures for ability levels one, two, and three. Procedures begin with strategies designed for level three students, continue with level two strategies, and conclude with level one strategies. Our definition of student ability at each ability level is as follows:

Level One: Good reading skills, ability to organize and interpret information from several sources with minimal direction from teacher, and ability to complete assignments independently.

Level Two: Average reading skills, ability to organize and interpret information from several sources with general direction from teacher, and ability to complete assignments with some assistance from teacher.

Level Three: Limited reading skills, and ability to organize and interpret information from several sources with step-by-step direction from teacher, and ability to complete assignments with close supervision from teacher.

These ability levels are merely guides. We recognize that you will adapt the exercises to suit your students' needs and your own teaching style.

Time Line

A time line is included for use by your students. Some exercises suggest that students consult the time line, so you may want to reproduce it for each student or display it.

Glossary and Brief Biographies

Some students will have difficulty reading these documents. To help them, we have included a glossary and brief biographies. The glossary provides definitions of specialized words or phrases used in the documents as well as some biographical entries and explanations of abbreviations frequently found in the documents. The biographies provide information about some of the people who appear in the documents.

Bibliography

As students work with the documents, they should be assigned appropriate readings from their textbooks and other secondary sources. They should also be encouraged to use the resources of school and public libraries. To guide them, an annotated bibliography appears at the end of the Teachers Guide. The selections were based on their appropriateness to the subject and their general availability through public and school library systems.

General Objectives

Upon successfully completing the exercises in this unit, students should be able to demonstrate the following skills using a single document:

➤ Identify factual evidence

➤ Identify points of view (bias and/or prejudice)

➤ Collect, reorder, and weigh the significance of evidence

➤ Develop defensible inferences, conclusions, and generalizations from factual information

Using several documents from this unit, students should be able to:

➤ Analyze the documents to compare and contrast evidence

➤ Evaluate and interpret evidence drawn from the documents

Outline of Classroom Exercises

World War I: The Home Front

Exercise 1
America Moves Toward War

Exercise 2
Women and the War Effort

Exercise 3
Uncle Sam Needs You

Exercise 4
Reactions to the Call

Exercise 5
When Johnny Comes Marching Home

List of Documents

Following the identifying information for each document reproduced in this unit, we have given the record group (RG) number in which the original can be found. Should you want copies of these documents or wish to refer to them in correspondence with us, give the complete archival citation, which is found in the appendix on page 48. **You may duplicate any of the documents in this unit for use with your students.**

Documents in *World War I: The Home Front* are taken from the following record groups: Bureau of Employment Security (RG 183), Bureau of the Public Debt (RG 53), Committee on Public Information (RG 63), Department of Justice (RG 60), Department of Labor (RG 174), Immigration and Naturalization Service (RG 85), National Archives Collection of Donated Materials (RG 200), Office of the Chief Signal Officer (RG 111), Public Health Service (RG 90), United States Food Administration (RG 4), United States House of Representatives (RG 233), United States Railroad Administration (RG 14), United States Senate (RG 46), War Department General and Special Staffs (RG 165), and Women's Bureau (RG 86).

1. Petition of United Mine Workers of America, March 29, 1917 (RG 46).

2. Circular letter from Congressman John F. Carew, March 7, 1916 (RG 233).

3. Letter to Secretary of Labor from President of Howard University, March 26, 1917 (RG 174).

4. News clipping from *The Washington Post*, February 1, 1917 (RG 174).

5. Letter to Secretary of Labor from National Woman's Peace Party, March 30, 1917 (RG 174).

6. Petition of the Business Men's Association of Towanda, PA, December 7, 1915 (RG 46).

7. Resolution of the General Assembly of Rhode Island, February 23, 1916 (RG 46).

8. Photograph, "Women packing soldiers' comfort kits at the American Overseas Committee," 1918 (RG 165).

9. Photograph, "Members of the 'Women's Land Army' laboring on a farm at Newton Square, Pennsylvania," 1918 (RG 165).

10. Photograph, "Female factory office workers volunteering to pack bandages for the American Red Cross," New Britain, CT, February 10, 1919 (RG 165).

11. Photograph, "Women workers in munitions plant, Gray & Davis Co.," Cambridge, MA, January 14, 1919 (RG 111).

12. Photograph, "Students at Mt. Holyoke College learning agricultural duties," South Hadley, MA, August 20, 1918 (RG 165).

13. Photograph, Ordnance Manufacture, Lancaster, PA, n.d. (RG 165).

14. Photograph, "Community Food Demonstration," May 25, 1918 (RG 165).

15. Photograph, "Federal Home Demonstration," Omaha, NE, June 1918 (RG 165).

16. Letter to the Bureau of Women in Industry from the ACME Die-Casting Corporation, October 23, 1918 (RG 86).

17. Letter to Wisconsin State Railway Commission from Mrs. Myrtle Altenburg, August 27, 1918 (RG 14).

18. Letter to State Factory inspector from Valley Cotton Oil Company, October 15, 1918 (RG 86).

19. Woman in Industry Service Standards, n.d. (RG 86).

20. Press Release No. 81 concerning food conservation, "Stop Eating Soldiers!", January 15, 1918 (RG 4).

21. Flyer, "The Day's Most Important Messages," Committee on Public Information, n.d. (RG 63).

22. Flyer, "Ways To Do Something for Your Country," National Committee of Patriotic Societies, n.d. (RG 63).

23. "The Daily German Lie," Committee on Public Information, n.d. (RG 63).

24. Poster, "Beat Back the Hun with Liberty Bonds," Third Liberty Loan n.d. (RG 53).

25. Poster, "Food Will Win the War," Food Administration n.d.(RG 4).

26. Poster, "Sure! We'll Finish the Job," Victory Liberty Loan, n.d. (RG 53).

27. Poster, "Team Work Wins," Food Administration, n.d. (RG 4).

28. Letter from C. Ludwig Schonberg to Acting Director of Internment, February 18, 1918 (RG 85).

29. Letter from Max Eastman, editor of the magazine, *The Masses*, to the public, n.d. (RG 60).

30. Letter from E. E. Brewer to Congressman Haugher, April 8, 1918 (RG 233).

31. Letter from United States Attorney's Office, New York, to Attorney General, Washington, DC, concerning Max Eastman, November 30, 1917 (RG 60).

32. Letter from A. D. Leyhe to Justice Department, December 5, 1918 (RG 60).

33. Letter from W. J. Payne concerning activities of Rose Pastor Stokes, September 25, 1918 (RG 60).

34. Newspaper clipping concerning speech made by Rose Pastor Stokes, September 25, 1918 (RG 60).

35. Letter from Lazarus Davidow to President Wilson, September 18, 1918 (RG 60).

36. Letter from Charles B. Johnson to Secretary of Labor, November 5, 1917 (RG 174).

37. Letter from John Gunlach to Honorable W. B. Wilson, July 28, 1917 (RG 174).

38. Photograph, "Soldiers mustering out of Army," n.d. (RG 165).

39. Photograph, "Group of emigrants waiting for arrival of ship," Southhampton, England, n.d. (RG 90).

40. Photograph, "Women's suffrage protestor with sign," November 19, 1918 (RG 165).

41. Painting by Jacob Lawrence, "Negro Migration," n.d. (National Archives Collection of Donated Materials).

42. U.S. Employment Service chart (July 1918-June 1919) (RG 183).

43. Letter from J. T. Watkins to W. B. Wilson, July 14, 1917 (RG 174).

44. Memorandum from the Director of Negro Economics Division to the Assistant Secretary of Labor, March 18, 1921 (RG 174).

45. U.S. Department of Labor report, December 5, 1918 (RG 174).

46. Dr. Anna Howard Shaw's article from *Carry On* (publication of Women's Committee, Council of National Defense), December 21, 1918 (RG 74).

47. Letter from George A. Kennedy to Secretary of Labor, n.d. (RG 174).

Introductory Exercises

These exercises introduce students to the general objectives of the unit. They focus students' attention on documents and their importance to historians, who interpret and record the past. We encourage you to use one or more of them as opening exercises for this unit.

Written Document Analysis

The Written Document Analysis worksheet helps students to analyze systematically any written document in this unit. In sections 1-5 of the worksheet, students locate basic details within the document. In section 6 students analyze the document more critically as they complete items A-E. There are many possible correct answers to section 6, A-E. We suggest you use document 1 with this worksheet to introduce your students to the nature of documents and their role in the development of history.

Photograph Analysis

The Photograph Analysis worksheet helps students to identify systematically the historical evidence within photographs. It is designed to improve students' ability to use photographs as historical documents. It can be used specifically with documents 8-15 and 38-41.

Poster Analysis

The Poster Analysis worksheet helps students to analyze systematically any poster in this unit. It is designed to improve students' ability to analyze the visual and written information contained in posters. It can be used specifically with documents 24-27.

Written Document Analysis

Worksheet

1. Type of Document (Check one):
   - _____ Newspaper
   - _____ Letter
   - _____ Patent
   - _____ Memorandum
   - _____ Map
   - _____ Telegram
   - _____ Press release
   - _____ Report
   - _____ Advertisement
   - _____ Congressional record
   - _____ Census report
   - _____ Other

2. Unique Physical Qualities of the Document (check one or more):
   - _____ Interesting letterhead
   - _____ Handwritten
   - _____ Typed
   - _____ Seals
   - _____ Notations
   - _____ "RECEIVED" stamp
   - _____ Other

3. Date(s) of Document: _____

4. Author (or creator) of the Document: _____

   Position (Title): _____

5. For What Audience was the Document Written? _____

6. Document Information (There are many possible ways to answer A-E.)

   A. List three things the author said that you think are important:

      1. _____
      2. _____
      3. _____

   B. Why do you think this document was written?

      _____

      _____

   C. What evidence in the document helps you to know why it was written?
      Quote from the document.

      _____

      _____

   D. List two things the document tells you about life in the United States
      at the time it was written:

      1. _____
      2. _____

   E. Write a question to the author that is left unanswered by the document:

      _____

      _____

Designed and developed by the education staff of the National Archives and Records Administration, Washington, DC 20408.

Photograph Analysis

Worksheet

Step 1. Observation

   A. Study the photograph for 2 minutes. Form an overall impression of the photograph and then examine individual items. Next, divide the photo into quadrants and study each section to see what new details become visible.

   B. Use the chart below to list people, objects, and activities in the photograph.

PEOPLE	OBJECTS	ACTIVITIES
_____	_____	_____
_____	_____	_____
_____	_____	_____
_____	_____	_____
_____	_____	_____
_____	_____	_____

Step 2. Inference

Based on what you have observed above, list three things you might infer from this photograph:

   1. _____

   2. _____

   3. _____

Step 3. Questions

   A. What questions does this photograph raise in your mind?

      _____

      _____

   B. Where could you find answers to them?

      _____

      _____

Designed and developed by the education staff of the National Archives and Records Administration, Washington, DC 20408.

Poster Analysis

Worksheet

1. What are the main colors used in the poster?

   _____

   _____

2. What symbols (if any) are used in the poster?

   _____

   _____

3. If a symbol is used, is it

   _____

   _____

   a. clear (easy to interpret)?

   _____

   _____

   b. memorable?

   _____

   _____

   c. dramatic?

   _____

   _____

4. Are the messages in the poster more visual or verbal?

   _____

   _____

5. Who do you think is the intended audience for the poster?

   _____

   _____

6. What does the government hope that the audience will do?

   _____

   _____

7. What purpose(s) of government are served by the poster?

   _____

   _____

8. The most effective posters use symbols that are unusual, simple, and direct. Is this an effective poster?

   _____

   _____

Designed and developed by the education staff of the National Archives and Records Administration, Washington, DC 20408.

Exercise 1
America Moves Toward War

Note to the Teacher

The exercises for this topic are designed to introduce the study of America's role in World War I. The simulation activities will engage the imagination of your students about the attitudes of the American people prior to our entry into the war.

The documents selected for the activities are typical of materials found in the correspondence files of congressional committees and the Department of Labor during the years prior to America's entry into the war. They were chosen because they are personal statements of citizens and because they mirror aspects of the public mood.

As your students work with the documents, they may raise questions that you will wish to address as you study the war. Or, students might use these questions as the focus for an independent research project.

The time line will serve as a very useful tool for you and your students with these exercises. Post it on your bulletin board so that students may refer to it as necessary.

Time: Variable

Objectives:

- Identify specific factors that influenced American public attitudes toward entry into World War I and weigh the significance of these factors.

- List specific events that influenced American attitudes toward the European war, 1914-17.

- List methods by which the American public communicated with its government.

Materials Needed:

Documents 1-7
Six personality sketches
Time line

Procedures:

1. To set the stage for studying World War I, you might hold a general class discussion about one or several of these general issues: (a) For what reasons do nations enter into conflict? (b) What part does the general population play in making the decision to enter a war? (c) What are the effects of war on the population of a country? (d) What are some of the changes caused by a war? Into what categories do these fall? (e) What might entry into a war today mean to you and your family? (f) What do you know about World War I? What would you like to know? If you keep a list of the students' ideas, this might serve as a basis for an evaluation of the unit at its conclusion.

a. Divide the class into small groups of three to five students.

b. Assign one document to each group. There are seven different documents.

c. Instruct each group to read its document carefully and to be prepared to explain to the class who wrote the document, when it was written, and what the opinion of the writer(s) was toward American neutrality.

d. To assist the groups, place this chart on the chalkboard:
    Author
    Date
    Type of document
    Opinions stated

e. If students have trouble reading the documents, help them by reviewing the text with them paragraph by paragraph.

f. Each group should select a recorder to complete the chart. Or, you may wish to duplicate the chart as a worksheet for each student.

g. As a culminating activity, ask the students what generalizations they can safely draw about public opinion toward America's entry into the war based on the evidence in the documents or on prior knowledge that they can support. As they develop their generalizations, be sure that they distinguish carefully between generalizations based on this evidence and generalizations unsupported by this evidence.

2. As an alternative to activity 1, you might set the stage as described in #1 above and then proceed as follows.

a. Assign one personality to each student or to a small group of students.

b. Make the documents available to the students to read carefully. The documents may be circulated among the class or placed in a resource center. Students may not find it necessary to use all the documents in forming their opinions.

c. Ask each student to write a letter either to William J. Stone (D-MO), Chairman of the Senate Foreign Relations Committee, or to George E. Chamberlain (D-OR), Chairman of the Senate Military Affairs Committee, stating opinions on the neutral stance of the United States. Stress that students' arguments should be based on evidence (or conclusions drawn from that evidence) found within the documents and the personality sketch.

d. The time line will be useful to students to determine a date for the letter and therefore a point of view. For example, a letter written before the publication of the Zimmermann Telegram might differ greatly from one written after that event. (For a digitized copy of the Zimmermann Telegram, log on the Digital Classroom section of the National Archives web site at **www.nara.gov/education** and click on "Primary Sources and Activities.")

e. When students have finished writing their letters, review the personalities for the class and ask students to share the letters. Ask members of the class to comment on whether or not they found the arguments logical and convincing.

3. As a second alternative, you might set the stage as described in #1 above and then proceed with the following activities.

a. Assign one personality to each student or to a small group of students.

b. Ask each student or group to prepare for a public meeting to consider the issue of

American neutrality from the perspective of the individual described in the personality sketch. The date of the meeting is April 1917.

c. Make the documents available to the students to read carefully. The documents may be circulated among the students or placed in a resource center. Students may not find it necessary to use all the documents in forming their opinions.

d. Point out to the students that their arguments must be logically based on the perspective of the individual described in the personality sketch. Students may want to focus their thoughts on "personal reasons," "business interests," "political ideas," and the like. Clues for these attitudes will be found within each personality sketch. Sample questions about each personality are provided at the end of each sketch. Students should be prepared to have their opinions challenged by their classmates.

e. After the students have had time to review the documents, convene the public meeting and request statements on the issue of American neutrality from the participants.

f. *Meeting ground rules:* To keep the discussion moving, you may want to serve as the moderator. Also, you may want to outline briefly information about each personality on the chalkboard. Each speaker should identify himself or herself to the class. If the class has worked in small groups, ask one student to serve as speaker for each group. Members of each group should be prepared to provide support for the statements of the group's speaker. As a culminating activity for the meeting, you might hold a vote on America's role or draft a resolution similar to that of Rhode Island.

4. Extended activities

a. Invite students to keep their personality sketches and note in a journal how that person's perspective might change as the war proceeds.

b. Expressing opinions to the government can be done in a variety of ways. Ask students to investigate the methods used to communicate with the government and then compose a letter expressing their opinions on a particular issue to the appropriate government agency or official.

c. Ask students to put together "documentation" of a current issue from as many sources as possible. They might hold a "public meeting" similar to activity 3, focusing on that issue. Then ask them to imagine what future occurrences would change their opinions regarding the issue.

d. During the Vietnam War, many Americans actively protested the involvement of the United States in the war. Ask students to locate information about opposition to American involvement in World War I and share that information with the class. Students might also compare the opposition to World War I with the protest demonstrations during the 1960s and 1970s. See the bibliography for information.

e. The draft was imposed for the second time in American history during World War I. Ask students to find out why the draft was established and to examine how it was received by the American public. Consult the bibliography.

Personality Sketches

Milton Gordon. You are a 41-year-old African American. You migrated from Natchez, MS, to Chicago, IL, and from there to Milwaukee, WI. You left Natchez because the boll weevil destroyed your cotton crop and you were unable to find another job. In Wisconsin you earn $1,400 a year making cigars in a factory. You are a widower with four sons ranging in age from 17 to 9. To boost the family income, your 17-year-old son earns $682 folding newspapers and your 15-year-old son earns $429 selling them. Another member of the family is your 61-year-old uncle. He served in the 25th Colored Infantry (established after the Civil War). He was dishonorably discharged from military service for his alleged participation in a race riot, and you are his sole means of support.

1. How might war affect the cigar-making business?

2. How might Mr. Gordon's family situation affect his attitudes toward entering the war?

3. What might be his uncle's attitudes toward the war?

Matthew Wright. You are a lawyer by profession, working primarily with the overseas investment section of a major bank in Richmond, VA. Two years ago you were elected to the Richmond City Council for the first time. You campaigned as a progressive candidate and as a friend to business. You are a veteran of the Spanish-American War. You have a wife and four children: two daughters, 12 and 18, and two sons, 14 and 20.

1. How might the war affect Mr. Wright's political stance?

2. How might Mr. Wright's job affect his attitudes?

3. As a supporter of business, what might Mr. Wright think of entry into the war?

4. How do you think the fact that Mr. Wright was a veteran of the Spanish-American War would affect his attitudes?

Thaddeus Franckt. You emigrated from Germany to the United States in 1899, leaving behind your father and two brothers. You became an American citizen in 1907. You came to America with no skills or money. Today you are a skilled machinist with a small manufacturing company in Detroit, MI. You are 45 years old, married with three children: two girls, 12 and 14, and one boy, 16. Recently you have been made foreman of the shop, a position you have worked very hard to attain. The company is facing hard times and many of your subordinates have been laid off. They have expressed their displeasure at a "foreigner's" promotion. You are very aware that their protests may jeopardize your job.

1. How might war affect a small company's business?

2. How might war affect Mr. Franckt's job with the company? How might his co-workers feel?

3. How might the war affect Mr. Franckt's family?

James Masters. You are a principal salesman for Eastman Kodak Company, Rochester, NY. You serve as the international sales representative for Kodak. You travel extensively throughout the world, especially in Western Europe. You have just returned from a trip to Northern Europe and are disappointed at the prospects for further trade during the course of the war. You are married, 47 years old, with no children. Your wife often accompanies you on your business trips. She is an artist, and you especially enjoy visiting the historical sights and museums throughout Europe.

1. How might the war affect Mr. Masters' job?

2. How might war affect the Eastman Kodak business?

3. What might be Mrs. Masters' attitudes toward entry into the war?

Roger Anderson. You are a 21-year-old graduate of Stanford University in California. You majored in economics. While attending Stanford, you worked occasionally as an accountant for a small accounting firm. The firm hopes to expand its business and has offered you a part-time accounting position with prospects for becoming full-time, depending on business. You are engaged to a classmate, Susan Williams, who is completing her studies to become a nurse. You plan to be married as soon as both of your professional futures are secure. Susan has been very active in the Women's Peace Party.

1. As a Californian, how might Roger feel about entering the European war?

2. How might the war affect Roger's and Susan's careers?

3. What influence might Susan have on Roger?

Emma Walker. You are a school teacher in Clarion, Iowa, a farming community in central Iowa. You are 31 years old, and you live at home with your parents. You have been teaching for the last 6 years in a one-room school with children of all ages. You are saving your small salary to move to Des Moines, the capital city, to pursue a job with the city school system. Your father has been a farmer for the last 40 years. He raises corn and has a small number of cattle. Your two older brothers also farm in the Clarion vicinity. They both have small farms of their own, are married, and are raising their own families.

1. How might the war affect Ms. Walker's job prospects?

2. What effect might the war have on the Walker family?

3. What effect might the war have on farmers in Iowa?

4. As a woman, how might Ms. Walker feel about the war?

Exercise 2
Women and the War Effort

Note to the Teacher

The documents and activities provided with this topic give students the chance to look closely at the roles that women assumed during the war and the effect of the war on their lives. The letters are typical of those sent by women or their employers to the Department of Labor.

The photographic documentation will provide students with another experience in developing their historical research skills. Like written documents, photographs are records. They provide information, they record activities, and they create a record of those activities for the future. Their use as historical materials requires historical skills. As they study the photographs, students will focus on identifying the factual information in them, concentrating on collecting visual details; they will make inferences about them and generalize from them.

Generalizations from photographs, as from written sources, tend to be more valid as the sample increases; depending on the quality of the sources, a generalization from ten items illustrating one idea is likely to be more valid than a generalization from one item. It is important for you and your students to know that these photographs were chosen from hundreds like them and that they represent typical activities that women engaged in during the war.

Time: 1-2 class periods

Objectives:

- Identify details in a photograph and describe their importance to the subject of the photo.

- Identify women's contributions to the war on the home front.

- Describe in detail the nature of women's roles in the war effort.

Materials Needed:

Documents 8-19
Photograph Analysis worksheet
Glossary

Procedures:

1. As an opening discussion before distributing the photographs, ask students to describe what they think everyday life was like for both men and women in the United States in 1917. Consider modes of transportation, dress styles, entertainment, types of employment, and the like. Next, consider how life might have been changed by entry into the war. Then ask students to imagine what roles women might have assumed as a result of the war effort (include volunteer activities). List these roles on the chalkboard; for example, nurse, worker in a job left by a soldier, Red Cross volunteer, and others.

a. When the students have completed their list of roles, select one and consider carefully what it might be like for a woman to assume that role. To stimulate students' imaginations, ask them to focus on these questions: What might a woman wear while doing that task? Where might that job be done? What might the working conditions be like? Would men be doing the same job? How are the women aiding the war effort? Time permitting, discuss these questions for several of the roles identified by the class.

b. Form eight small groups and distribute one of the photographs (documents 8-15) and a Photograph Analysis worksheet to each group.

c. Using the worksheet as a guide to analyzing the photograph, ask each group to prepare a summary of the activities shown in the photograph. Ask them what they learn about everyday life and the role of women in 1917 by looking at the photo. To be thorough, they will need to focus on specific details within the photograph and to consider such elements as modes of dress, location of job, expressions of patriotism, welfare of workers, sanitary conditions, roles of men, support of the war effort, "modern" conveniences, and purpose of the photograph.

d. When the groups have completed their summaries, ask them to share their photograph and ideas with the entire class.

e. Review the original list of roles placed on the chalkboard and compare it with the evidence in the photographs. It should become apparent to students that the photographs are a very valuable form of evidence when looking at the past, particularly in terms of detailed evidence. What differences do these details make in students' thinking?

f. As a culminating activity or homework assignment, ask students to write a paragraph describing in some detail the role of women on the home front. These assignments should draw heavily on the photographic evidence reviewed by the class.

2. Divide your class into three groups. Duplicate copies of documents 16-18 and distribute to the three groups. Place the following chart on the chalkboard and ask each group to complete it with information from its letter.

- Who wrote the letter?
- To whom?
- When was the letter written?
- What was the purpose of the letter?
- Does the author make a clear "case"?
- How might you reply to this letter?
- Make a list of your ideas.

Ask each group to select a reporter to summarize its findings (contained on the chart) for the entire class.

Conclude this activity by duplicating and distributing document 19 to students. Review the standards with the class and discuss the role of the government in setting such standards for industry. Ask each group to consider how the government might reply to its letter.

2

3. Extended activities

    a. Ask students what they think the government's current attitude is toward working women. Ask them where they might obtain this information, and to suggest which governmental agencies have been created to deal with women's issues.

    b. Assign a group of students to develop a time line of significant events relating to working women from 1914 to today.

    c. Ask for volunteers to compile photographs that illustrate how women's roles at work have changed and display them in the classroom.

    d. After World War I, women gained the right to vote. Ask one or two students to investigate the effects the war had on this movement and report their findings to the class. Suggest that they consult other documents in this unit and the bibliography.

    e. Display a series of photographs from current newspapers and magazines and ask students to speculate on the value of this evidence for future historians.

Exercise 3
Uncle Sam Needs You

Note to the Teacher

This exercise focuses on the efforts of the federal government to communicate with the American people during World War I. Using a variety of techniques, the government attempted to enlist the active support of citizens at home "to do their bit for the boys over there."

Comparisons between these initial efforts of the government to mobilize public support for the war and current media campaigns by government agencies (ranging from anti-smoking efforts to energy conservation) will provide students with a valuable sense of historical perspective. The final activities for each exercise involve students in defining "propaganda" as well as recognizing its techniques.

Please note that some of the documents employ words that will be unfamiliar to students. You might wish to develop a vocabulary exercise for students before working with the materials.

Time: 2 class periods

Objectives:

- Identify methods used by the government during World War I to communicate with American citizens.
- Develop working definitions of "propaganda."
- Identify the techniques used by an author to persuade the reader of a particular point of view.
- Write an example of a persuasive argument.
- Compare and contrast written samples of informative and persuasive styles.
- Identify the message of a poster and the techniques used to convey this message.

Materials Needed:

Documents 20-27
Worksheet 1
Poster Analysis worksheet
Glossary

Procedures:

1. Duplicate copies of student worksheet 1 for the class. Make available to the class several copies of documents 21-23. Divide the class into small groups of 3 to 5 students and assign a document to each group.

   a. Ask each group to use its document to complete the worksheet. After the worksheets are finished, ask students to share their findings with the class.

   b. As a culminating activity, ask students to develop a definition of "propaganda" based on the ideas discussed in the worksheet.

3

2. Before displaying the posters (documents 24-27), ask students to list methods that might have been used during World War I to inform the public about the war effort and enlist its support. Record these ideas on the chalkboard.

    a. Ask students to rank these methods in order of their effectiveness as sources of information for the public.

    b. Display the posters and ask students whether or not they think posters were important to the war effort. This issue may have been raised in your opening discussion.

    c. Duplicate and distribute copies of the Poster Analysis worksheet for each student. Direct them to complete the worksheets for the posters they selected.

    d. When the worksheets have been completed, ask students to report their findings.

    e. As a final discussion, ask students to consider the following:

        1) Who might have developed such a poster campaign and why? What is your evidence?

        2) What evidence is there that the posters were designed to inform the American public of the government's war efforts?

        3) What evidence is there that the posters were designed to persuade the American public to support the government's war efforts?

        4) When do you think persuasion is an appropriate role for the government? Can you cite examples?

        5) Do you think a poster campaign would be an effective method of informing or persuading the public today? Why or why not?

3. Duplicate copies of document 20. Before examining the document, make sure that students understand the purpose of a press release. Write the following questions on the chalkboard and divide the class into small groups to answer them.

    a. What do you think the author means by the title "Stop Eating Soldiers!"?

    b. According to the press release, what can you do at home to aid the war effort?

    c. Restate in your own words: "Democracy is equally menaced by gluttony and Germany."

    d. What is the attitude of the author toward women and their role in the war effort?

After a discussion of the students' responses, ask each student to write two paragraphs to convince the reader of his or her stance on a particular issue. The first paragraph should be written in an informative style with emphasis on the factual information. The second paragraph should be written in a persuasive style similar to "Stop Eating Soldiers." This might be a joint assignment with an English teacher.

As a concluding discussion, review several of the paragraphs and discuss the techniques used in both approaches. How are they different? What are the tools of persuasion? Why are these tools used?

4. Extended activities

    a. Ask students to collect and bring to class contemporary conservation materials and compare with "Stop Eating Soldiers." As they share their collections, ask the students to explain whether they think the items they have collected are more or less effective in conveying their messages than the posters examined.

    b. Assign students to make a list of television advertisements in which the government is trying to convince them of something (public service spots relating to automobile safety, voter registration, and the like) and, in a oral report, compare these with commercial advertisements in terms of the tools of persuasion used.

    c. Using the "America Moves Toward War" documents (1-7) in this unit, students should compare and contrast citizens' efforts to communicate with the government and vice versa.

    d. Conduct a class discussion on this question: What controls should the government impose on the media during a national crisis?

    e. Ask students to research and write a report comparing and contrasting mass media presentations developed during both World Wars and the Vietnam War.

    f. Select an issue around which students wish to develop a propaganda campaign; e.g., vegetarianism, school prayer amendment, better school lunches. Students should make an effort to employ several techniques (posters, photographs, letters, polls, flyers) and present their projects to the class or to another appropriate audience.

    g. Ask students to select a contemporary issue of concern, review periodicals (current and back issues) and television and radio commentary and advertisements about the subject, and write a report comparing and contrasting the forms in which government and private institutions couch propaganda and the uses to which they put it.

3

Uncle Sam Needs You

Worksheet 1

Directions: Use the information in documents 20-23 to complete this worksheet.

1. What audience is the government addressing in this document?

2. What is the message of the document?

3. Why do you think the government used this kind of document to convey its message?

4. In this document, does the government define "patriotism"? If so, how?

5. What is your personal reaction to the government's appeal?

6. List some ways the government communicates with you or your parents.

Exercise 4
Reactions to the Call

Note to the Teacher

The documents in this exercise illustrate a wide range of reactions to the war and war related issues. While students may readily identify the behavior of individuals and/or groups, you should call to their attention the fact that implicit within the documents are the policies and practices of the federal government.

The worksheets and extended class activities provided are designed to help students identify the facts and recognize any inferences, generalizations, or conclusions that they draw from them. Both activities require that documents 28-37 and worksheets 2-5 be distributed among four groups. Activity 1 is designed to help students identify channels used by citizens to show their disapproval or support for the government and the war. In activity 2 students are asked to identify some of the people and organizations in the documents; to classify actions as patriotic, treasonous, democratic, or tyrannical; and to explain the assumptions behind their classifications.

Time: 2-4 class periods

Objectives:

- Identify specific reactions (individual and institutional) to the war effort.

- Identify channels used by American citizens to express support or disapproval of the government and the war.

- Develop working definitions of "patriotism," "treason," "democracy," and "tyranny."

- Classify activities (individual and institutional) according to the definitions they have developed.

Materials Needed:

Worksheets 2-5
Documents 28-37
Glossary
Brief biographies

Procedures:

1. Introduce the topic by leading a class discussion focusing on the following:

   a. List methods (e.g., petitioning, demonstrating, lobbying, terrorizing) people use to express their opinions about wars and other government actions.

   b. List factors that influence a person's attitude toward war.

   c. What are some of the ways American citizens expressed their support or disapproval of World War I as seen in the documents from other topics in this unit?

4

Divide the class into four groups and distribute the materials as follows:

	DOCUMENTS	WORKSHEET
Group One	28-30	2
Group Two	31 & 32	3
Group Three	33-35	4
Group Four	36 & 37	5

Ask students to consider the issues raised in the opening discussion as they work with the documents.

Then list the following items on the chalkboard. Ask one student from each group to write a brief identification beside the names of people or organizations represented in the documents the group examined.

a. C. Ludwig Schonberg (document 28)

b. E. E. Brewer (document 30)

c. A. D. Leyhe (document 32)

d. Max Eastman (documents 29 & 31)

e. Lazarus Davidow (document 35)

f. Detroit Police (document 35)

g. American Protective League (document 35)

h. W. J. Payne (document 33)

i. Rose Pastor Stokes (documents 33, 34, & 35)

j. Charles B. Johnson (document 36)

k. Hoboken Piers (document 37)

Finally, ask members of each group to respond to the following:

a. What methods of showing support or disapproval of the war effort appear in the documents examined? What factors appear to influence attitudes toward the war effort (political affiliation, ethnic background, and the like)?

b. What can you conclude about the types of people or organizations that supported/opposed the war effort? Be sure to cite evidence from the documents that supports your conclusions.

c. Is there any information in the identifications (a-k) that is not purely factual? If so, what is the basis of the information?

d. How do you think your own biases or prejudices affect your answers to the worksheet questions? Give examples.

2. Conduct a class discussion in which students develop definitions of "patriotism," "treason," "democracy," and "tyranny." Begin with dictionary definitions. To assist students, suggest that they classify as patriotic, treasonous, democratic, and tyrannical the following activities: voting, burning the flag, resisting the draft, displaying the flag on national holidays, driving 55 mph, government wiretapping, and establishing national health care. Discuss with students the differences in their classifications.

Using the same grouping and materials as described in exercise 1, ask students to consider the issues raised in the opening discussion as they work with the documents.

Each group should decide on definitions of "patriotism," "treason," "democracy," and "tyranny" and to cite examples of these in the documents. Students will in effect define behavior and events in relation to their own attitudes, and, like historians, they must always be aware of the extent to which personal biases affect their historical judgments.

When the worksheets have been completed, ask each group to make a presentation based on information in the documents examined. (Groups may prepare oral reports, create role-play situations based on activities in the documents, and the like.) Group presentations should include the following:

a. Identification of people and organizations in the documents.

b. Evidence from the documents used to classify activities as patriotic, treasonous, democratic, and tyrannical.

c. Information about how students' personal prejudices or biases may have affected judgments made of the people and events in the documents.

d. Specific indications of the basis of the information presented (personal reactions, facts, inferences, generalizations, or conclusions).

Ask the class to comment on the group presentations, noting particularly the way in which the group classified the activities in the documents.

3. Extended activities: Assign students one of the following research topics for a written report.

a. Violations of the Espionage and Selective Service Acts.

b. Socialist antiwar activities for the 1914-19 period.

c. Government justification for the suspension or violation of certain civil rights during wartime; e.g., Lincoln's suspension of writ of habeas corpus for secessionists during the Civil War, World War I internment of Germans, World War II Japanese relocation.

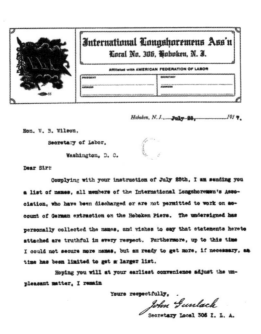

Exercise 4: Reactions to the Call

Worksheet 2

Directions: Use the information in the documents to answer these questions.

Documents 28, 29, & 30

1. Record factual information in each document, such as date of writing, subjects, authors, and persons or groups addressed.

2. What are your personal reactions to each of the letters? Are you sympathetic or unsympathetic? Why or why not?

Document 28

3. Who was C. Ludwig Schonberg? To whom was he writing and why?

Document 29

4. Who was Max Eastman? To whom was he writing and why?

Document 30

5. Who was E. E. Brewer? To whom was he writing and why?

Exercise 4: Reactions to the Call

Worksheet 3

Directions: Use the information in the documents to answer these questions.

Documents 31 & 32

1. Record factual information in each document, such as date of writing, subjects, authors, and persons or groups addressed.

Document 31

2. Why was Max Eastman being prosecuted?

3. Describe your personal reaction to the quotation from Max Eastman's article.

Document 32

4. Why had the Russian group been jailed?

5. What was the purpose of A. D. Leyhe's letter?

6. Are you sympathetic or unsympathetic to the request? Why or why not?

7. Does the fact that the United States was at war affect your judgment of Max Eastman and/ or the Russians? Why or why not?

Exercise 4: Reactions to the Call

Worksheet 4

Directions: Use the information in the documents to answer these questions.

Documents 33, 34, & 35

1. Record factual information in each document, such as date of writing, subjects, authors, and persons or groups addressed.

Document 33

2. What is W. J. Payne's complaint about Mrs. Stokes?

Document 34

3. The newspaper clipping attached to Mr. Payne's letter contains a quote from one of Mrs. Stokes' speeches. Identify any information in that quote or anything about the way it is written that might suggest to you what her political affiliation was.

Document 35

4. What did the Detroit Police Department and the American Protective League do? Why do you think they took such action?

5. What was Lazarus Davidow's opinion about actions of the Detroit Police Department and the American Protective League? Do you agree or disagree?

6. In your opinion did Mrs. Stokes have the right to oppose the war program? Why or why not?

Exercise 4: Reactions to the Call

Worksheet 5

Directions: Use the information in the documents to answer these questions.

Documents 36 & 37

1. Record factual information in each document, such as date of writing, subjects, authors, and persons or groups addressed.

Document 36

2. What was Mr. Johnson's concern? To whom was he writing and why?

3. Is there information in the letter about the status of black people in 1917?

Document 37

4. Who was being fired from Hoboken Piers? Why?

5. What do you learn about the employees from reading the brief descriptions of them?

6. If you had been the manager of Hoboken Piers, would you have fired these men? If so, how would you have justified your action?

Exercise 5
When Johnny Comes Marching Home

Note to the Teacher

The information in these documents mostly relates to employment of immigrants, women, African Americans, and returning soldiers at the close of the war. But the material also reflects information about the social attitudes and the expectations of these and other people, as well as information about the attitudes and function of the government agencies responsible for their welfare.

Included in this exercise are three types of documents that students will use to examine the postwar situation: photographs, textual materials, and a chart. The U.S. Employment Service chart requires mathematical analysis. If you find that the chart is too difficult or frustrating for your students, eliminate it and assign group one members to work in other groups. If you choose to use the chart, you might make a calculator available to the students.

Time: 1-2 class periods

Objectives:

- Identify some of the problems and issues confronting Americans at the close of the war.

- Develop a classification system for postwar issues and problems.

- Develop their own criteria for extracting historical information from documents to use in writing statements about postwar problems and issues.

Materials Needed:

Documents 38-47
Worksheets 6-10

Procedures:

1. Circulate the photographs (documents 38-41) to the class and ask students to identify the subject of each.

2. Discuss these questions with students: What effects might the war have had on each of the groups in the photographs? What problems or issues might the groups have had to face as a result of the war's ending?

3. Divide the class into five groups and distribute the materials as follows:

	DOCUMENTS	WORKSHEET
Group One	42	6
Group Two	43 & 44	7
Group Three	45	8
Group Four	46	9
Group Five	47	10

4. Based on class discussion and information from the documents and worksheets, direct the class to develop a chart categorizing problems related to the end of the war. The students might list problems and/or issues in one column; origins or causes in a second; and possible solutions, effects, or results in a third. Ask students to note the basis of charted information (facts, inferences, generalizations, and conclusions).

5. Focus the closing discussion around the following questions:

   a. What was the basic concern of each of the four groups of people in the documents that you examined?

   b. What were the attitudes of government agencies toward the groups they served? What is the evidence from these documents?

   c. To what extent are many post-World War I problems still with us? How are they the same or different?

   d. What sources of information do students use to answer the above (fact, inference, generalization, conclusion)?

6. Extended activities: Students may be asked to do further research on the following:

   a. One or several of the postwar concerns dealt with in the documents, such as women or immigration policies.

   b. Postwar issues not dealt with in the documents, such as prohibition, women's suffrage and other civil rights movements, the Red Scare, or the Roaring 20s.

   c. A comparison of the return of the Vietnam veteran with the return of the World War I soldier.

Students should consider very carefully the effect of the war on any of these issues and consider the extent to which many of the post-World War I issues they examine are still with us today.

Exercise 5: When Johnny Comes Marching Home

Worksheet 6

Directions: Use information in the document to answer these questions.

Document 42

1. What kind of document is this?

2. Who produced it?

3. When was it produced?

4. What kind of information can you get from it?

5. Using the scale, establish the approximate number of workers applying and the number of workers placed each month from July 1918 through June 1919.

6. Based on the information above, can you determine in which month(s) the U.S. Employment Service was most successful in placing workers? Why or why not?

7. Determine mathematically in which month(s) the U.S. Employment Service was most successful in placing workers.

8. What conclusions about the employment situation from July 1918 through June 1919 can you draw from this chart? Refer to the time line and the glossary as needed.

9. By whom might charts such as this be used and why?

Exercise 5: When Johnny Comes Marching Home

Worksheet 7

Directions: Use information in the documents to answer these questions.

Documents 43 & 44

1. What kinds of documents are these? Who wrote them? To whom are they written? What are the subjects of each?

2. List reasons why large numbers of African Americans were migrating to the North.

3. What problems were caused by this migration?

4. What kinds of jobs might have been found in the North? (Consider the dates of the documents.)

5. How might African American migration be affected by the end of the war?

Document 44

1. What is a memorandum? Establish your definition from this document.

2. What is the purpose of the memorandum?

3. To whom is it addressed?

4. To which of the problems in document 43 is the memorandum directly related?

5. What are some proposed solutions to the problem suggested in the memorandum?

6. Is there evidence in this memorandum that mass migration did not result only from the war?

7. Is there in the memorandum evidence that migration continued to be an issue after the war?

8. Is there information in the memorandum that reveals anything about the attitude of the author or the government toward African Americans? Explain.

Exercise 5: When Johnny Comes Marching Home

Worksheet 8

Directions: Use information in the document to answer these questions.

Document 45

1. What kind of document is this? Who is the author? To whom is it written? What is the subject?

2. For what reasons did returning soldiers have difficulty finding employment?

3. What is the name of the agency that was responsible for helping them find jobs?

4. What were some of the other responsibilities of that agency?

5. What appears to be the attitude of the agency toward the soldiers? Support your answers.

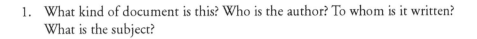

Exercise 5: When Johnny Comes Marching Home

Worksheet 9

Directions: Use information in the document to answer these questions.

Document 46

1. What kind of document is this? Who is the author? To whom is it written? What is the subject?

2. What roles had women assumed during the war? (For additional information, see exercise 2, "Women and the War Effort.")

3. What is Dr. Shaw's message? To whom is it addressed?

4. Why do you think the article was written?

5. What is the tone of the article?

5

Exercise 5: When Johnny Comes Marching Home

Worksheet 10

Directions: Use information in the documents to answer these questions.

Document 47

1. What kind of document is this? Who is the author? To whom is it written? What is the subject?

2. Why might the letter have been written to the Secretary of Labor?

3. What are the author's complaints about immigrants?

4. What particular group does he attack?

5. Describe in your own words the author's attitudes toward immigration. What does this reveal about your attitude toward immigration in the 1914-19 period?

6. Is there any information in the letter that might give you a clue about the Secretary of Labor's attitude toward immigration? Explain.

7. What particular immigrant groups might have suffered the most discrimination as a result of the war?

Time Line

1914	April 9	Mexican troops board U.S.S. *Dolphin*, an American dispatch boat, in Tampico, Mexico.
	April 21	American troops seize the Veracruz, Mexico, custom house and occupy city.
	June 28	Archduke Francis Ferdinand, heir to the Austro-Hungarian throne, assassinated by Serbian nationalist.
	August 4	European war declared, United States declares neutrality.
	August 19	(America will be) "...impartial in thought as well as deed." President Woodrow Wilson.
	November 3	Britain declares the North Sea a military area and sets mines. The North Sea was a major shipping lane at the time.
1915	February 4	Germany declares area around Britain a war zone, threatens to shoot on sight, and declares that neutrals enter at own risk.
	February 10	United States delivers "note" to Germany protesting violation of neutral rights.
	March 11	British blockade of German ports.
	March 28	*Falaba* sunk; 1 American dead.
	May 1	*Gulflight*, American tanker, sunk; 2 Americans dead.
	May 7	*Lusitania* sunk; 128 Americans dead.
	July 24	Briefcase Spy Affair (New York), evidence of German espionage in America.
	August 19	*Arabic* sunk; 2 Americans dead.
	September 1	*Arabic* pledge: Germans pledge not to sink liners without providing for the safety of noncombatants. Ships warned not to try to escape.
	December 4	Henry Ford leaves New York on "Peace Ship" to seek peace in Europe.
1916	February	McLemore Resolution in Congress, warning Americans not to travel on armed vessels. President Wilson opposes this resolution and pledges to defend the "rights" of Americans as neutrals to travel the seas.
	February 29	Germans announce intention to attack armed merchant ships without warning.
	March 10	Pancho Villa raids Columbus, NM. Gen. John Pershing sent to capture Villa.
	March 24	Germans violate *Arabic* pledge by sinking *Sussex*.
	May 4	*Sussex* pledge: Germans agree not to sink unresisting merchant or passenger liners without warning.
	June 3	Passage of National Defense Act, expanding the regular army.
	June 10	The Republican Convention nominates Charles Evans Hughes for President.
	June 16	The Democratic Convention renominates Woodrow Wilson for President.
	July 30	Munitions plant explosion, Black Tom Island, NJ. German sabotage is suspected.
	August 29	Establishment of Council of National Defense to coordinate industry and resources for national security.
	November 7	Wilson wins re-election on campaign slogan "He kept us out of war."
1917	January 22	President Wilson declares American interest in European "Peace Without Victory."
	February 1	German high command institutes unrestricted submarine warfare.

	February 3	Sinking of the *Housatonic* without warning. United States breaks diplomatic relations with Germany.
	February 5	Pershing's Mexican Expedition ended.
	February 5	Revision of immigration laws to include literacy provision. First major general restriction to immigration flow into the United States.
	March	Revolution in Russia, Alexander Kerensky's Provisional Government created. Tsar overthrown.
	March 1	Zimmermann Note, a German message to Mexico offering parts of United States to Mexicans if they join the war with Germany, revealed to press.
	March 1	Passage of Armed Ship Bill to arm merchant marine ships in order to deter submarines.
	March 22	United States recognizes new Russian government.
	April 2	Wilson's speech to Congress asks for declaration of war.
	April 6	Wilson signs joint resolution declaring war.
	April 6	President issues proclamation outlining the rights and restrictions of resident aliens, particularly German Americans, and establishes basis for their internment.
	April 14	Creation of Committee on Public Information to disseminate information on war to publishers of newspapers and periodicals.
	April 17	*Smith* attacked by German submarine, first military action against the United States.
	April 24	Passage of Liberty (Emergency) Loan Act to finance war.
	May 18	Passage of Selective Service Act to draft men, ages 21-30.
	June 15	Espionage Act establishes penalties for anti-American activities.
	June 26	First U.S. troops arrive in France.
	July 28	Creation of War Industries Board to coordinate industries nationwide.
	August 10	Food and Fuel Act creates agencies to coordinate food and fuel supplies nationwide.
	October 3	War Revenue Act creates income tax to support war effort.
	October 6	Trading With the Enemy Act forbids commerce with enemy nations. The Office of Alien Property is created to hold German-owned businesses.
	November 6-7	Bolshevik Revolution in Russia brings Lenin to power.
	December 18	Eighteenth Amendment (Prohibition) passed by Congress. Ratified by states, January 1919.
	December 26	Establishment of U.S. Railroad Administration to coordinate railroad transportation nationwide.
1918	January 8	President Wilson sets out Fourteen Points for peace to Congress.
	March 3	Treaty of Brest-Litovsk between Germany and Russia ends war on eastern front.
	Spring	Major German offensive on western front. Push to end war.
	April 5	Creation of War Finance Corporation to finance war industries.
	April 8	Establishment of National War Labor Board to control labor conditions and disputes.
	May 16	Sedition Act amends Espionage Act. Under provisions of Sedition Act, Socialist leader Eugene V. Debs is arrested. On September 14, Debs is sentenced to 10 years in prison.

	May 20	Overman Act gives President broad powers to reorganize executive offices.
	September 30	Bulgaria surrenders to Allies.
	November 3	Mutiny of German Navy at Kiel, catalyst for revolution in Germany.
	November 4	Austria surrenders.
	November 7	Revolution in Germany.
	November 9	Kaiser abdicates and flees Germany.
	November 11	Armistice signed.
	December 4	Wilson departs for Versailles Peace Talks.
1919	**January 18**	Opening of Peace Conference.
	February 14	Covenant of League of Nations drafted.
	June 28	Treaty of Versailles signed.

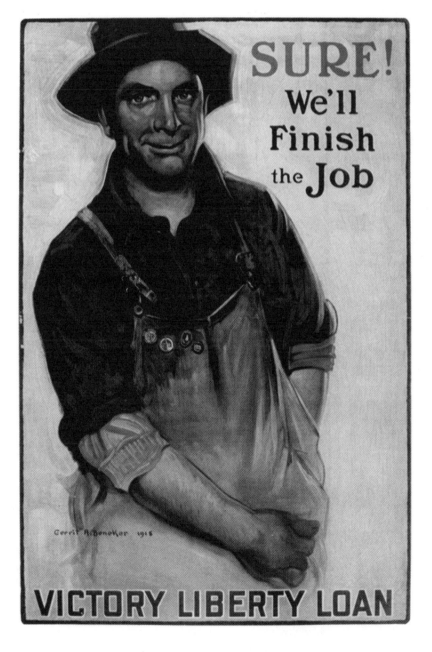

Glossary

Allied and Associated Powers

The 21 nations (led by the United States, Great Britain, France, Russia, Italy, and Japan) that opposed the Central Powers in World War I.

American Protective League

A volunteer civilian organization operating under the supervision of the Justice Department. This group was placed at the disposal of the War Department, Military Intelligence Division.

Berlin

The capital and military headquarters of Germany during World War I.

Central Powers

The combined nations that opposed the Allied and Associated Powers in World War I, including Germany, the Austro-Hungarian Empire, Turkey, and Bulgaria.

Committee on Public Information

President Wilson created the Committee on Public Information (CPI) in April 1917. The Committee, headed by Denver newspaperman George Creel, was charged with the responsibility of enlisting the support of the American people behind the war effort. The Committee produced such publications as *The Official Bulletin*, "The Daily German Lie," and countless pamphlets asking for the public's support of the war effort. The CPI also organized the "Four Minute Men" (identified below).

Conscription

A policy that requires military service to a country. The Selective Service Act, which authorized conscription, was passed May 18, 1917. (Also known as the draft.)

Contraband

Materials that could be used in war, such as munitions, steel, gunpowder, fuel, and other raw materials.

Council of National Defense

Established August 29, 1916, to coordinate resources and industries for national security and welfare. It consisted of six Cabinet members: the Secretaries of War, Navy, Interior, Agriculture, Commerce, and Labor. It was the first large emergency agency of World War I.

East St. Louis Riot (1917)

A riot that resulted from wartime industry recruiting southern African Americans to work in competition with white laborers.

Four Minute Men

A voluntary national organization begun by the Committee on Public Information. Members spoke before public gatherings promoting the sale of liberty loan bonds. The name of the group was derived from the length (4 minutes) of their speeches.

Influenza

A worldwide epidemic, 1918-19; 500,000 Americans died.

Internment

Confinement of enemy aliens during the war. This policy was established April 6, 1917.

Kaiser

The king of Germany, Wilhelm II (1888-1918).

Liberty Loans

In order to obtain the necessary funds for the conduct of the war, the U.S. Treasury borrowed money through a series of bond issues. The first four bonds issued were known as "Liberty Loans" and the fifth bond as the "Victory Loan."

Munitions

Materials used in war; weapons and ammunition.

Neutral

A person or government not taking part or giving assistance in a dispute or war between others.

Press Release

A statement prepared for and distributed to the press.

Propaganda

A planned effort to shape people's ideas and opinions generally in support or opposition to a cause.

Socialist Party

Founded in 1901, the Socialist Party of America was an influential force in American politics until after World War I. Its leader, Eugene V. Debs, received almost a million votes in the presidential election of 1912. Torn by bitter internal fighting between those who favored gradual reform of the capitalist system and those who favored more radical action, the party split into three parts in 1919 and ceased to be a significant factor in American politics.

U-boat

German submarine.

U.S. Employment Service

Established on January 3, 1918, to direct immigrants (later, all persons) to likely employment. During World War I, it served as the exclusive recruiting agency of unskilled labor for all industries except farms, railroads, and nonessential industries that could recruit labor for themselves. After the war, it assisted discharged soldiers, sailors, and civilian workers in locating employment.

U.S. Railroad Administration

Established on December 26,1917, under the authority of the Army Appropriation Act of August 29, 1916. President Wilson was given full control of railroads on December 28, 1917. The Railroad Administration was subsequently authorized to control railway express companies and inland waterway systems. The office functioned until 1937.

Victory Parade

Community-sponsored parades to welcome returning troops. Some 200,000 troops marched in 450 parades.

Women in Industry Service

Created in 1918 to develop standards and policies to ensure the effective employment of women in the labor force while protecting their "health and welfare."

Brief Biographies

BAKER, NEWTON D. After serving as city solicitor and mayor of Cleveland, OH, Baker became President Wilson's Secretary of War in 1916. In spite of his dislike of the military and his reputation as a pacifist, he was responsible during his tenure in the War Department for sending troops to Mexico to pursue Pancho Villa, drafting tens of thousands of young men into the service, and administering the expenditure of $15 billion for the war.

BARUCH, BERNARD. Wealthy financier who served as chairman of the War Industries Board. In that capacity, he exercised great power and responsibility in mobilizing American industry for the war effort. Later he served as an adviser to Franklin D. Roosevelt.

BRYAN, WILLIAM JENNINGS. After three unsuccessful campaigns as Democratic candidate for President, Bryan became Wilson's Secretary of State in 1913. Highly moralistic and idealistic, he pleaded for a policy of strict neutrality toward the belligerents. He resigned as Secretary of State in protest to President Wilson's harshly worded note to Germany after the sinking of the *Lusitania* in 1915.

CREEL, GEORGE. A former reporter and editor, Creel played a prominent role as a writer and speaker in Wilson's election campaign of 1916. After the United States entered the war, he headed the Committee on Public Information, which zealously distributed propaganda to the news media to win popular support for the war effort.

DANIELS, JOSEPHUS. North Carolina editor and publisher who ardently supported Wilson's presidential nomination in 1912. As Secretary of the Navy from 1913 to 1921, he supervised the Navy's preparation for and operations during the war. His Assistant Secretary of the Navy was a then obscure politician, Franklin D. Roosevelt.

DEBS, EUGENE V. Charismatic labor leader who organized the Social Democratic Labor Party of America in 1897 and who ran as Socialist Party candidate for President five times between 1900 and 1920. Debs' outspoken opposition to America's entry into the war led to his imprisonment for violation of the Espionage Act of 1917.

EASTMAN, MAX. Noted poet, lecturer, and editor born in 1883. In 1910 he organized the Men's League for Women's Suffrage, the first such men's organization. From 1913 to 1917 he edited the Socialist magazine *Masses*. He later became a critic of Marxism in his writings and lectures.

FRANKFURTER, FELIX. Famed attorney, Harvard University law professor, and Supreme Court Justice. During the war, he was chairman of the War Labor Policies Board, which ensured that an adequate number of workers was available in key industries to meet the needs of the war.

HOOVER, HERBERT. Self-made millionaire who won worldwide acclaim for directing relief efforts in war-torn Belgium in 1914 and 1915. After U.S. entry into the war, Wilson appointed him to head the Food Administration to increase production and supervise distribution of the nation's food supplies. Later became U.S. President (1929-33).

HOUSE, EDWARD. A Texan who was instrumental in Wilson's nomination in 1912. Although he refused a Cabinet post, in an unofficial capacity he became Wilson's closest and most trusted adviser. House made several unsuccessful trips to Europe while America was still neutral in order to work out a negotiated settlement of the war acceptable to both sides.

LANSING, ROBERT. Expert in international law who became Secretary of State in 1915 after Bryan's resignation. Although Lansing was not personally close to Wilson, he exercised considerable influence in persuading the President to act firmly toward Germany. Served as Secretary of State until 1920.

LODGE, HENRY CABOT. Senator from Massachusetts who became Republican floor leader in 1918 and played a key role in defeating Wilson's plan for a League of Nations after the war.

McADOO, WILLIAM G. Lawyer, railroad magnate, and Senator from California who worked diligently for Wilson's nomination in 1912. He served as Wilson's Secretary of the Treasury and married his daughter, Eleanor, in 1914.

SCOTT, EMMETT JAY. Served as special assistant to the Secretary of War to advise in matters affecting African American soldiers, 1917-19. Prior to that appointment, he served as secretary to Booker T. Washington and as secretary-treasurer at Howard University, Washington, DC. He published two books, *The American Negro in the World War* and *Negro Migration During the War*.

SHAW, ANNA HOWARD. Minister, medical doctor, lecturer, and, from 1904 to 1915, president of the National American Woman Suffrage Association. During the war, she chaired the Woman's Committee of the U.S. Council of National Defense, in which she coordinated the various functions carried out by women for the war effort.

STOKES, ROSE HARRIET PASTOR. A leader of the American Socialist Party and a prolific writer of articles, reviews, poems, and plays. When the United States entered World War I, she withdrew from the Socialist Party because of its opposition to the war. But she soon changed her mind, rejoined the party, and was arrested for violation of the Espionage Act. Her offense was writing to a newspaper: "I am for the people, while the Government is for the profiteers."

WILSON, WILLIAM B. Born in 1862 in Scotland, Wilson immigrated to the United States in 1870. He was a member of the National Executive Board, which organized the United Mine Workers of America in 1890. From 1907 to 1913, when President Wilson appointed him first Secretary of Labor, he served as a member of the U.S. Congress.

WILSON, WOODROW. Former president of Princeton University and Governor of New Jersey who was elected President of the United States on a reform platform in 1912. Wilson expected to concentrate on domestic issues as President, but to his dismay, foreign crises persistently monopolized his attention. A stern moralist and fervent idealist, he led the United States into World War I with great reluctance but with hope of establishing a world free of war and aggression.

Annotated Bibliography

The following books are recommended to provide background for you and your students on the varied American attitudes toward World War I and the changing roles played by the federal government as a result of American involvement in the war.

Barbeau, Arthur E. and Henri, Florette. *The Unknown Soldiers*. New York: Da Capo Press, 1996.

>A careful study of African American participation in World War I. Much of the book deals with black troops in Europe. The first two chapters cover the effects of American involvement upon blacks on the home front, including migration to northern cities and various attitudes of blacks toward the war. The last chapter deals with the black soldier's questioning of his status as a second-class citizen even after the war's end.

Baruch, Bernard M. *The Public Years*. New York: Holt, Rinehart and Winston, 1960.

>Bernard Baruch served as head of the War Industries Board during much of America's involvement in World War I. The first five chapters of his autobiography deal with these years. Baruch's book includes many personal anecdotes, making it interesting reading. The chapter on the War Industries Board provides a good, brief description of that agency's function.

Bristow, Nancy K. *Making Men Moral: Social Engineering during the Great War.* New York: New York University Press, 1996.

>The history of a federal program to maintain high standards of moral purity at military training bases, this work discusses the national government's effort to ensure that good soldiers were also solid citizens.

Child, Clifton James. *The German-Americans in Politics, 1914-1917*. New York: Arno Press, 1970.

>A well-researched history of the German-American Alliance, a political and cultural organization supporting and encouraging German-American traditions, during World War I. Many teachers may discover the text too detailed for their use and will find short articles in other sources more helpful. However, for the teacher who is particularly interested in the attitudes of German-Americans during the war, this book is strongly recommended.

Churchill, Allen. *Over Here! An Informal Re-creation of the Home Front in World War I*. New York: Dodd, Mead & Company, 1968.

>An excellent study of this country during the war years, reflecting the changing attitudes of Americans toward U.S. involvement. The book is lively and will appeal to students in late junior high and high school.

Clarke, Ida Glyde. *American Women and the World War*. New York: D. Appleton and Company, 1918.

>Written immediately after the Armistice, the book provides a very patriotic view of the work done by women to further the war effort. The table of contents includes brief descriptions of the material covered in each chapter, simplifying selected reading for the teacher. Chapter X, "Women in Industry," is of particular interest.

Clarkson, Grosvenor B. *Industrial America in the World War: The Strategy Behind the Lines, 1917-1918*. New York: Houghton Mifflin Company, 1923.

>Detailed account of the War Industries Board, America's final phase of industrial mobilization for World War I, written shortly after the Armistice. Each chapter is briefly outlined in the table of contents, allowing the teacher to focus quickly on selected topics. Suggested for teachers.

Creel, George. *How We Advertised the War*. New York: Harper & Brothers Publishers, 1920.

> Written immediately after the war by the director of the Committee on Public Information, the book is an interesting account of the techniques used to sell America's involvement in a European war to her own people. The first five chapters contain Mr. Creel's defense of the actions of his Committee. The rest of the book discusses poster campaigns, movies, speakers bureaus, and similar devices used to stimulate patriotism during the period. Suggested for teachers.

DuPuy, Ernest R. *Five Days to War, April 2-6, 1917*. Harrisburg, PA: Stackpole Books, 1967.

> An interesting account, well supplemented by photographs, of events, social conditions, and attitudes in America leading to U.S. entry into World War I. The text is casual in style, appropriate for late junior high and early senior high school students.

Early, Frances H. *A World without War: How U.S. Feminists and Pacifists Resisted World War I*. Syracuse, NY: Syracuse University Press, 1997.

> By explaining the alliance between feminists and pacifists during World War I, Early touches on many of the social aspects of the war and their effects on the American home front. In addition, this work also addresses how the U.S. government responded to dissent during wartime, balancing its commitment to the war effort with cherished American civil liberties.

Flexner, Eleanor. *Century of Struggle*. Cambridge, MA: Belknap Press of Harvard University Press, 1996.

> A detailed account of the women's rights movement in the United States from the founding of the colonies until the ratification of the 19th amendment. Chapters XX and XXI deal with the movement during the war years and are of particular interest to teachers.

Graham, Otis L., Jr. *The Great Campaigns: Reform and War in America, 1900-1928*. Malabar, FL: R.E. Krieger Pub. Co., 1987.

> A brief account of the American social scene prior to entry into the war as well as a short political and diplomatic history of the war. This book provides a quick review for teachers before beginning the World War I unit.

Harries, Meirion and Susie Harries. *The Last Days of Innocence: America at War, 1917-1918*. New York: Random House, 1997.

> Covering both the American home front and the American military effort during World War I, this book shows how the war fundamentally transformed the United States, making it a world power and bringing the country squarely into the modern age.

Heck, Bessie Holland. *The Hopeful Years*. New York: The World Publishing Company, 1964.

> Novel concerning a teenage girl's growing up in the midwest during the early years of World War I. By today's standards, her life seems somewhat old fashioned, but the author's concern is with the effects of America's entry into the war on individual lives. Suggested for early junior high school students.

Hines, Walter D. *War History of American Railroads*. New Haven: Yale University Press, 1928.

> Walter Hines was director-general of railroads from 1919 to 1920. The introduction and first four chapters of his book deal with the state of the railroad system in America prior to our entry into World War I and the changes that occurred as a result of our involvement. The text is a detailed study of the railroads during war mobilization, including the federal government's role in that process. Suggested for teachers.

Jantzen, Steven. *Hooray for Peace; Hurrah for War*. New York: Facts on File, 1991.

> An informal description of the United States during World War I. The author has relied heavily upon newspaper and magazine stories, cartoons, photographs, and other primary sources of the period. His style reads easily and quickly. Suggested for junior high school students.

Jensen, Joan M. *The Price of Vigilance.* New York: Rand McNally & Company, 1968.

> An extensive study of the American Protective League, the volunteer organization that viewed itself responsible for the discovery of disloyal Americans during the war. The book is very detailed; however, the first several chapters may provide some very useful background material. Chapter 3, "Soldiers of Darkness," is of particular interest to those concentrating on the suppression of the radical labor movement during the war.

Kennedy, David M. *Over Here: The First World War and American Society.* New York: Oxford University Press, 1980.

> A major study of America's role in World War I, this book takes a hard look at how the war affected American society. In particular, Kennedy's work examines the expanding sphere of the federal government and its efforts to quash domestic dissent on a variety of topics in the name of patriotism and the war effort.

May, Ernest R. *The World War and American Isolation, 1914-1917.* Chicago: Quadrangle Books, 1966.

> A scholarly, well-documented account of events leading to America's entry into World War I by a distinguished historian. The book is very detailed. Suggested for the teacher who has a strong interest in the subject.

Mock, James R., and Larson, Cedric. *Words That Won the War.* New York: Russell & Russell, 1968.

> Originally published in 1939, this book recounts the history of the Committee on Public Information. The first few chapters will serve the teacher who wants a brief introduction to the Committee and its functions. The reader should keep in mind the state of affairs in this country and in Europe when the book was written. Perhaps that will shed some light upon the author's point of view.

Peterson, H. C. *Propaganda For War.* Port Washington, NY: Kennikat Press , 1968.

> A fascinating study of the effects of British propaganda upon American neutrality during the early years of World War I. For the teacher who wants only a brief introduction to the subject, chapters I, III, VIII, and XI are strongly recommended. The author's style is straightforward; consequently, the text reads quickly. Suggested for teachers.

Peterson, H. C., and Fite, Gilbert C. *Opponents of War, 1917-1918.* Westport, CT: Greenwood Press, 1986.

> Accounts of various groups opposed to the war from 1917 to 1918. Each chapter can stand alone and may be useful to the teacher who considers supplemental reading assignments for high school students. The style is straightforward and chapters are short, making the book attractive to students.

Scott, Emmett J. *Negro Migration During the War.* New York: Arno Press, 1969.

> Originally published in 1920, the text is a scholarly study of black migration patterns, their causes and ramifications, during World War I. Emmett Scott was secretary-treasurer of Howard University, Washington, DC, and his work is highly respected.

Sullivan, Mark. *Our Times, The United States, 1900-1925.* Vol. V: *Over Here, 1914-1918.* New York: Charles Scribner's Sons, 1933.

> An informal description of the domestic scene during World War I, written roughly a decade later. The author has included many fine photographs, cartoons, and newspaper clippings from the period. The material covered in each chapter is briefly outlined in the table of contents, facilitating the use of the book for selective reading by upper high school students and teachers.

Thomas, Norman. *Is Conscience a Crime?* New York: Vanguard Press, 1927.

> A defense of conscientious objectors written shortly after World War I, the book documents the "movement" during the war years. Of particular interest are chapters II-IV, dealing with the various groups of people who objected to the war on moral, social, or political grounds. Suggested for upper high school students and teachers.

Trask, David F., ed. *World War I at Home.* New York: John Wiley & Sons, Inc., 1970.

> Collection of short readings divided into three sections: neutrality (1914-17), belligerency (1917-18), and peacemaking (1919-20). The selections were taken from magazines, newspapers, and other publications printed during the war years and cover a variety of topics, including pacifism, mobilization, labor, and civil liberties. The book is highly recommended to the teacher who is interested in short readings for high school students.

Tuchman, Barbara W. *The Zimmermann Telegram.* New York: Macmillan, 1966.

> Exciting but sometimes wordy story of the Zimmermann affair. Ms. Tuchman has written a thrilling account of the events surrounding the interception and decoding of the ill-fated telegram sent to the Imperial German Minister in Mexico during World War I. Suggested for high school students.

Urofsky, Melvin I. *Big Steel and the Wilson Administration.* Columbus, OH: Ohio State University Press, 1969.

> Scholarly work concerning the relationship between the steel industry and the federal government during the Wilson era. Chapters III, V, and VI deal with the increased role of the government in mobilizing the industry during the war years. Suggested as background reading for teachers.

Werstein, Irving. *Over Here and Over There.* New York: W.W. Norton & Company, Inc., 1968.

> Brief description of life in the United States as well as happenings in Europe during the war years. The author has included many excellent photographs and political cartoons. Suggested for junior high school students.

Zieger, Robert H. *America's Great War: World War I and the American Experience.* Lanham, MD: Rowman & Littlefield, 2000.

> This work examines the political context of America's role in World War I, including international shipping and trade before 1917, the U.S. decision to enter the war, the effort to organize the American expeditionary force, and attempts to silence domestic dissent from labor groups and reformers.

World War I: The Home Front
Archival Citations of Documents

1. Petition of United Mine Workers Local 2819 speaking against the United States' entering World War I, March 29, 1917; Committee on Military Affairs; "Against Preparation for National Defense" (SEN65A-J39); 65th Congress; Records of the U.S. Senate, Record Group 46; National Archives Building, Washington, DC.

2. Circular letter from Congressman John Carew urging his constituents not to sail in the merchant vessels of belligerent countries, March 7, 1916; Committee on Foreign Affairs; "Sailing of U.S. Citizens" (HR64A-F13.3); 64th Congress; Records of the U.S. House of Representatives, Record Group 233; National Archives Building, Washington, DC.

3. Letter from the President of Howard University S.M. Newman to the Secretary of Labor offering services to the nation at a critical time, March 26, 1917; 16/431; Chief Clerk's Files; General Records, 1907-1942; General Records of the Department of Labor, Record Group 174; National Archives at College Park, College Park, MD.

4. Article from *The Washington Post* listing the sinkings of American vessels and the losses of American lives due to German submarine warfare, February 1, 1917; 16/439, Sundry Matters Relating to the War; Chief Clerk's Files, 16/429-16/442; General Records, 1907-1942; General Records of the Department of Labor, Record Group 174; National Archives at College Park, College Park, MD.

5. Letter from Mrs. Harold S. Buttenheim, state chairman of the New Jersey Division of the National Women's Peace Party, to the Secretary of Labor stating her party's opposition to the United States' joining the war, March 30, 1917; 9/273, Welfare of Women; Chief Clerk's Files; General Records, 1907-1942; General Records of the Department of Labor, Record Group 174; National Archives at College Park, College Park, MD.

6. Petition from the Business Men's Association of Towanda, PA, to the state's congressional delegation urging increases in the nation's defense preparedness, December 7, 1915; Committee on Military Affairs; (SEN64A-J56); 64th Congress; Records of the U.S. Senate, Record Group 46; National Archives Building, Washington, DC.

7. Resolution of the Rhode Island General Assembly urging Congress to increase the military and naval forces of the government, February 23, 1916; Committee on Military Affairs; "Favoring Preparedness for National Defense" (SEN 64A-J56); 64th Congress, 2nd Session; Records of the U.S. Senate, Record Group 46; National Archives Building, Washington, DC.

8. Photograph No. 165-WW-35B-10; "Women packing soldiers' comfort kits at the American Overseas Committee," 1918; Records of the War Department General and Special Staffs, Record Group 165; National Archives at College Park, College Park, MD.

9. Photograph No. 165-WW-581A; "Members of the 'Women's Land Army' laboring on a farm at Newton Square, Pennsylvania," 1918; Records of the War Department General and Special Staffs, Record Group 165; National Archives at College Park, College Park, MD.

10. Photograph No. 165-WW-35A-2; "Female factory office workers volunteering to pack bandages for the American Red Cross," New Britain, CT, February 10, 1919; Record of the War Department General and Special Staffs, Record Group 165; National Archives at College Park, College Park, MD.

11. Photograph No. 111-SC-31635; "Women workers in munitions plant, Gray & Davis Co.," Cambridge, MA, January 14, 1919; Records of the Office of the Chief Signal Officer, Record Group 111; National Archives at College Park, College Park, MD.

12. Photograph No. 165-WW-109A-1; "Students at Mt. Holyoke College learning agricultural duties," August 20, 1918; Records of the War Department General and Special Staffs, Record Group 165; National Archives at College Park, College Park, MD.

13. Photograph No. 111-SC-59342; Ordnance Manufacture, n.d.; Records of the War Department General and Special Staffs, Record Group 165; National Archives at College Park, College Park, MD.

14. Photograph No. 165-WW-174-6; "Community food demonstration," May 25, 1918; Records of the War Department General and Special Staffs, Record Group 165; National Archives at College Park, College Park, MD.

15. Photograph No. 165-WW-173-7; "Federal home demonstration," Omaha, NE, June 1918; Records of the War Department General and Special Staffs, Record Group 165; National Archives at College Park, College Park, MD.

16. Letter from ACME Die-Casting Corporation to Nelle Swartz, Chief of the Bureau of the Women in Industry, requesting permission to work female laborers overtime, October 23, 1918; Folder: ACME Die-Casting Corp.; Correspondence of the Director, 1918-1920, (A-M); Records of the Women's Bureau, Record Group 86; National Archives at College Park, College Park, MD.

17. Letter from Mrs. Myrtle Altenburg to the Wisconsin State Railway Commission requesting consideration for her working a railroad job for more than 10 hours per day, August 27, 1918; Complaint #8; Women's Service Section, 1918-1920, 227-237; Records of the Division of Labor, General Subject Files; Records of the United States Railroad Administration, Record Group 14; National Archives at College Park, College Park, MD.

18. Letter from the Valley Cotton Oil Company to Theodore Hoepfner, Tennessee State Factory Inspector, requesting permission to work female laborers on twelve-hour shifts, October 15, 1918; Folder: Valley Cotton Oil Company; Correspondence of the Director, 1918-1920, (S-Z); Records of the Women's Bureau, Record Group 86; National Archives at College Park, College Park, MD.

19. Women in Industry Service Standards, n.d.; Folder: Women in Industry Service; Correspondence of the Director, 1918-1920, (S-Z); Records of the Women's Bureau, Record Group 86; National Archives at College Park, College Park, MD.

20. Press release written by Herbert Kaufman in *Cosmopolitan* magazine, concerning food conservation ("Stop Eating Soldiers!"), January 15, 1918; 12HL-C3; Magazines, Featured Sections; Educational Division; Records of the U.S. Food Administration, Record Group 4; National Archives at College Park, College Park, MD.

21. Flyer, "The Day's Most Important Messages," released by the Committee on Public Information, n.d.; Folder 2: Advertising copies and layouts; Executive Division; Posters, layouts, and correspondence regarding advertising; File of Carl Byoir, Nov. 1917-June 1918, CPI-1-C6; Records of the Committee on Public Information, Record Group 63; National Archives at College Park, College Park, MD.

22. Flyer, "Ways to do something for your Country!" n.d.; National Committee of Patriotic Societies; Folder 2: Advertising copies and layouts; Executive Division; Posters, layouts, and correspondence regarding advertising; File of Carl Byoir, Nov. 1917-June 1918; CPI-1-C6; Records of the Committee on Public information, Record Group 63; National Archives at College Park, College Park, MD.

23. "The Daily German Lie," written by Harvey O'Higgins, Associate Chairman of the Committee in Public Information, n.d.; Information File used by Harvey O'Higgins in compiling the news services, CPI-1-C2; Records of the Committee on Public Information, Record Group 63; National Archives at College Park, College Park, MD.

24. Poster No. 53-WP-3B; "Beat Back the Hun with Liberty Bonds," n.d.; Third Liberty Loan; Records of the Bureau of the Public Debt, Record Group 53; National Archives at College Park, College Park, MD.

25. Poster No. 4-P-102; "Food Will Win the War," n.d.; Records of the U.S. Food Administration, Record Group 4; National Archives at College Park, College Park, MD.

26. Poster No. 53-WP-1C; "Sure! We'll Finish the Job," n.d.; Victory Liberty Loan; Records of the Bureau of the Public Debt, Record Group 53; National Archives at College Park, College Park, MD.

27. Poster No. 4-P-9; "Team Work Wins," n.d.; Records of the U.S. Food Administration, Record Group 4; National Archives at College Park, College Park, MD.

28. Letter from C. Ludwig Schonberg to the Acting Director of Internment requesting release from internment, February 18, 1918; 54261-132; Files regarding correspondence, Internment Camp, Hot Springs, NC; Records of the Immigration and Naturalization Service, Record Group 85; National Archives Building, Washington, DC.

29. Solicitation letter from Max Eastman, editor of the magazine *The Masses*, requesting financial support for his magazine, n.d.; File: 9-12-9; General Records of the Department of Justice, Record Group 60; National Archives at College Park, College Park, MD.

30. Letter from E.E. Brewer to Congressman Haugher requesting that the German language be banned in the United States, April 8, 1918; Committee on Education; "Banning of German Language" (HR65A-118.4); 65th Congress; Records of the U.S. House of Representatives, Record Group 233; National Archives Building, Washington, DC.

31. Letter from the U.S. Attorney's Office in New York to the Attorney General concerning a new indictment against Max Eastman, editor of magazine *The Masses*, November 30, 1917; File: 9-12-9; General Records of the Department of Justice, Record Group 60; National Archives at College Park, College Park, MD.

32. Letter from Attorney Albert Leyhe to the Department of Justice requesting the release of six Russian expatriates from military prisons after World War I, December 5, 1918; File: 186233-56; DJ Central Files, Straight Numerical Files, 186233-25 to 61; General Records of the Department of Justice, Record Group 60; National Archives at College Park, College Park, MD.

33. Letter from W.J. Payne regarding the activities of Rose Pastor Stokes, September 25, 1918; File: 9-19-1750; General Records of the Department of Justice, Record Group 60; National Archives at College Park, College Park, MD.

34. *New York Times* article about Rose Pastor Stokes commenting on the trial of Socialist Eugene Debs, September 25, 1918; File: 9-19-1750; General Records of the Department of Justice, Record Group 60; National Archives at College Park, College Park, MD.

35. Letter from attorney Lazarus Davidow to President Wilson protesting the violation of the rights of the audience at a lecture given by Rose Pastor Stokes in Detroit, September 18, 1918; File: 9-19-1750; General Records of the Department of Justice, Record Group 60; National Archives at College Park, College Park, MD.

36. Letter from Charles Johnson to the Secretary of Labor emphasizing the value of the colored labor force in supporting the nation's war effort, November 5, 1917; 8/102: Chief Clerk's Files; General Records, 1907-1942; General Records of the Department of Labor, Record Group 174; National Archives at College Park, College Park, MD.

37. Letter from John Gunlach, Secretary of International Longshoremen's Association Local 306, to the Secretary of Labor listing members of the local not permitted to work on the docks due to their German origins, July 28, 1917; 16/359; Chief Clerk's Files, 16/336-16/370; General Records, 1907-1942; General Records of the Department of Labor, Record Group 174; National Archives at College Park, College Park, MD.

38. Photograph No. 165-WW-139D-3; "Soldiers mustering out of Army," n.d.; Records of the War Department General and Special Staffs, Record Group 165; National Archives at College Park, College Park, MD.

39. Photograph No. 90-G-73-1; "Group of emigrants waiting for arrival of ship, Southhampton, England," n.d.; Records of the Public Health Service, Record Group 90; National Archives at College Park, College Park, MD.

40. Photograph No. 498-WW-600A-5; "Women's suffrage protestor with sign," November 19, 1918; Records of the War Department General and Special Staffs, Record Group 165; National Archives at College Park, College Park, MD.

41. Painting No. 200-HN-LA-1; "Negro Migration," by Jacob Lawrence, n.d.; part of Migration of Negroes Series; National Archives Collection of Donated Materials; National Archives at College Park, College Park, MD.

42. Chart showing relations between registrations, referred help, help wanted and place, by months, fiscal year 1919 in United States; 1st File: Box 1512; Records of the Office of Employment Secretary, Record Group 183; National Archives at College Park, College Park, MD.

43. Letter from Representative John T. Watkins to the Secretary of Labor complaining about the recruitment of Negro labor to the North, July 14, 1917; 8/102, Migration of Negroes North and East St. Louis Race Riots, 1917-1926; Chief Clerk's Files; General Records, 1907-1942; General Records of the Department of Labor, Record Group 174; National Archives at College Park, College Park, MD.

44. Letter from the Director of Negro Economics to the Assistant Secretary of Labor concerning the functions and work of the Negro Economics Advisory Service, March 18, 1921; 8/102D-9/181; Chief Clerk's Files; General Records, 1907-1942; General Records of the Department of Labor, Record Group 174; National Archives at College Park, College Park, MD.

45. Description of the Bureaus for Returning Soldiers and Sailors in the Department of Labor, December 5, 1918; 30/751; Chief Clerk's Files; General Records, 1907-1942; General Records of the Department of Labor, Record Group 174; National Archives at College Park, College Park, MD.

46. Dr. Anna Howard Shaw's article concerning the organization and mobilization of America's women from *Carry On*, publication of the Women's Committee (Michigan Division, Council of National Defense), December 21, 1918; 120/1A, Women's Bureau; Chief Clerk's Files; General Records, 1907-1942; General Records of the Department of Labor, Record Group 174; National Archives at College Park, College Park, MD.

47. Letter from George Kennedy to the Secretary of Labor regarding immigration policy, n.d.; 164/14; Chief Clerk's Files; General Records, 1907-1942; General Records of the Department of Labor, Record Group 174; National Archives at College Park, College Park, MD.

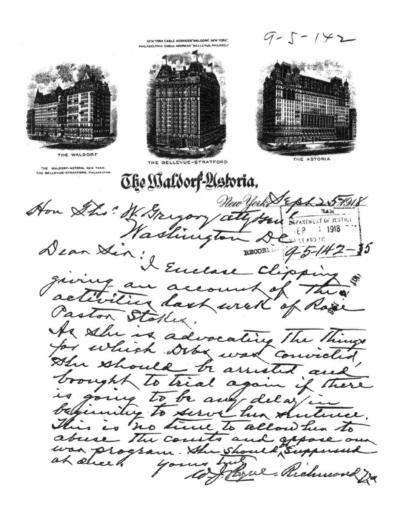

About the National Archives:
A Word to Educators

The National Archives and Records Administration (NARA) is responsible for the preservation and use of the permanently valuable records of the federal government. These materials provide evidence of the activities of the government from 1774 to the present in the form of written and printed documents, maps and posters, sound recordings, photographs, films, computer tapes, and other media. These rich archival sources are useful to everyone: federal officials seeking information on past government activities, citizens needing data for use in legal matters, historians, social scientists and public policy planners, environmentalists, historic preservationists, medical researchers, architects and engineers, novelists and playwrights, journalists researching stories, students preparing papers, and persons tracing their ancestry or satisfying their curiosity about particular historical events. These records are useful to you as educators either in preparing your own instructional materials or pursuing your own research.

The National Archives records are organized by the governmental body that created them rather than under a library's subject/author/title categories. There is no Dewey decimal or Library of Congress designation; each departmental bureau or collection of agency's records is assigned a record group number. In lieu of a card catalog, inventories and other finding aids assist the researcher in locating material in records not originally created for research purposes, often consisting of thousands of cubic feet of documentation.

The National Archives is a public institution whose records and research facilities nationwide are open to anyone 14 years of age and over. These facilities are found in the Washington, DC, metropolitan area, in the 11 Presidential libraries, the Nixon Presidential Materials Project, and in 16 regional archives across the nation. Whether you are pursuing broad historical questions or are interested in the history of your family, admittance to the research room at each location requires only that you fill out a simple form stating your name, address, and research interest. A staff member then issues an identification card, which is good for two years.

If you come to do research, you will be offered an initial interview with a reference archivist. You will also be able to talk with archivists who have custody of the records. If you have a clear definition of your questions and have prepared in advance by reading as many of the secondary sources as possible, you will find that these interviews can be very helpful in guiding you to the research material you need.

The best printed source of information about the overall holdings of the National Archives is the *Guide to the National Archives of the United States* (issued in 1974, reprinted in 1988), which is available in university libraries and many public libraries and online at **www.nara.gov**. The *Guide* describes in very general terms the records in the National Archives, gives the background and history of each agency represented by those records, and provides useful information about access to the records. To accommodate users outside of Washington, DC, the regional archives hold microfilm copies of much that is found in Washington. In addition, the regional archives contain records created by field offices of the federal government, including district and federal appellate court records, records of the Bureau of Indian Affairs, National Park Service, Bureau of Land Management, Forest Service, Bureau of the Census, and others. These records are particularly useful for local and regional history studies and in linking local with national historical events.

For more information about the National Archives and its educational and cultural programs, visit NARA's Web site at **www.nara.gov**.

Presidential Libraries

Herbert Hoover Library
210 Parkside Drive
West Branch, IA 52358-0488
319-643-5301

Franklin D. Roosevelt Library
511 Albany Post Road
Hyde Park, NY 12538-1999
914-229-8114

Harry S. Truman Library
500 West U.S. Highway 24
Independence, MO 64050-1798
816-833-1400

Dwight D. Eisenhower Library
200 Southeast Fourth Street
Abilene, KS 67410-2900
785-263-4751

John Fitzgerald Kennedy Library
Columbia Point
Boston, MA 02125-3398
617-929-4500

Lyndon Baines Johnson Library
2313 Red River Street
Austin, TX 78705-5702
512-916-5137

Gerald R. Ford Library
1000 Beal Avenue
Ann Arbor, MI 48109-2114
734-741-2218

Jimmy Carter Library
441 Freedom Parkway
Atlanta, GA 30307-1498
404-331-3942

Ronald Reagan Library
40 Presidential Drive
Simi Valley, CA 93065-0600
805-522-8444/800-410-8354

George Bush Library
1000 George Bush Drive
P.O. Box 10410
College Station, TX 77842-0410
409-260-9552

Clinton Presidential Materials Project
1000 LaHarpe Boulevard
Little Rock, AR 72201
501-254-6866

National Archives Regional Archives

NARA-Northeast Region
380 Trapelo Road
Waltham, MA 02452-6399
781-647-8104

NARA-Northeast Region
10 Conte Drive
Pittsfield, MA 01201-8230
413-445-6885

NARA-Northeast Region
201 Varick Street, 12th Floor
New York, NY 10014-4811
212-337-1300

NARA-Mid Atlantic Region
900 Market Street
Philadelphia, PA 19107-4292
215-597-3000

NARA-Mid Atlantic Region
14700 Townsend Road
Philadelphia, PA 19154-1096
215-671-9027

NARA-Southeast Region
1557 St. Joseph Avenue
East Point, GA 30344-2593
404-763-7474

NARA-Great Lakes Region
7358 South Pulaski Road
Chicago, IL 60629-5898
773-581-7816

NARA-Great Lakes Region
3150 Springboro Road
Dayton, OH 45439-1883
937-225-2852

NARA-Central Plains Region
2312 East Bannister Road
Kansas City, MO 64131-3011
816-926-6272

NARA-Central Plains Region
200 Space Center Drive
Lee's Summit, MO 64064-1182
816-478-7079

NARA-Southwest Region
501 West Felix Street
P.O. Box 6216
Fort Worth, TX 76115-0216
817-334-5525

NARA-Rocky Mountain Region
Denver Federal Center, Building 48
P.O. Box 25307
Denver, CO 80225-0307
303-236-0804

NARA-Pacific Region
24000 Avila Road
P.O. Box 6719
Laguna Niguel, CA 92607-6719
949-360-2641

NARA-Pacific Region
1000 Commodore Drive
San Bruno, CA 94066-2350
650-876-9009

NARA-Pacific Alaska Region
6125 Sand Point Way, NE
Seattle, WA 98115-7999
206-526-6507

NARA-Pacific Alaska Region
654 West Third Avenue
Anchorage, AK 99501-2145
907-271-2443

Reproductions of Documents

Reproductions of the oversized print documents included in these units are available in their original size by special order from Graphic Visions.

Frostburg Maryland
March 29th 1917

Whereas, The interests of the great toiling masses are never served by any war, and the interests of the toiling masses of this Country cannot possibly be in any way served by this Country entering the conflict which is now devastating the old world, and

Whereas, War has been proven the most expensive, unjust and ineffective means of settling disputes, therefore be it

Resolved, That Local Union No. 2819, United Mine Workers of America stands unalterably against war, not only as a general principal, but in this present crisis, and be it further

Resolved, That we stand unequivocably by the provisions of the U. S. constitution dealing with the rights of free speech, free press, and free assemblage, and call upon the people to demand that Congress refrain from tinkering in any manner with these constitutional rights of the American People.

Whereas, Militarism is contrary to the spirit of democracy, submersive of free popular government and institutions, and inculcates the war like spirit, therefore be it further

Resolved, That we express ourselves as unalterably opposed to the inauguration of compulsory military training in state or nation, and against conscription of any sort. And, be it further

Resolved, That we oppose Military Training in the public schools and colleges of the United States.

Speaking from our faith in democracy as well as from our hope of peace, we demand that in this as in all other crises, no matter how grave the provocation, the question of war and peace, most vital of all questions in the life of a nation, be submitted to the people by a national advisory referendum, before Congress declares war.

John E Davies
John Barber } *comitey*
Noah S Fuigg

Document 1. Petition of United Mine Workers of America, March 29, 1917. [National Archives]

JOHN F. CAREW, M.C.   Seventeenth District

   Tel. 1009 Plaza   New York.

311 East 57th Street

   New York City.

                    HOUSE OF REPRESENTATIVES,

                    WASHINGTON.

                                              March 7, 1916.

Sir:

        As your Congressman I feel it my duty to write to you as follows:

        Although it is one of the rights of an American Citizen to travel
abroad upon the merchant ships of the belligerent nations in the
present war, a right which neither the President nor Congress can or
should surrender, it is a right the exercise of which to-day is
entirely unnecessary and may possibly involve the Government and the
people of the United States in serious diplomatic difficulties and
may even in its consequences involve us in war.

        I think that an American Citizen who travels on one of such ships
is guilty of a treasonable disregard of the supreme patriotic duty
which every man owes to his country, never to imperil her peace and
happiness. So far as I am concerned I will be inclined to regard with
indifference the fate of a man who disregards this warning.

        If you have to go to sea, go in an American Ship. If you don't
have to go, stay home. At all times and in all places do all you can
to keep our beloved country out of danger. Remember your duties to
your country as well as your rights.

        "May Columbia ride safe through the Storm."

                              Yours truly,

                    (Signed)   JOHN F. CAREW.

Document 2. Circular letter from Congressman John F. Carew, March 7, 1916. [National Archives]

HOWARD UNIVERSITY
WASHINGTON, D.C.
PRESIDENT'S OFFICE

March 26, 1917.

The Secretary of Labor,
Washington, D. C.

Sir:

At a crowded assembly held in Howard University at noon today the following minute was unanimously and enthusiastically adopted:--

"We, officers, teachers, and students of Howard University, because of our unfailing devotion to our country, do hereby offer ourselves to her in mind, body, and estate for whatever use she may be able to make of us in maintaining her integrity and her high position among the nations of the world."

We wish to make plain by this statement that we hold ourselves ready as Americans for whatever we may be able to contribute to the Government of the United States in this critical time.

Yours sincerely,

J. M. Newman
President.

Death Harvest of Germany's Submarines Under Restrictions

Below is a partial record of the destruction of life and property resulting from Germany's submarine warfare, which Berlin claimed was in accordance with international law, before and after the pledge given to the United States September 1, 1915. What will be the result of the new policy of ruthlessness, of which the United States received warning yesterday:

SHIPS SUNK BY GERMAN SUBMARINES BEFORE PLEDGE TO UNITED STATES.

Name. Date.	Lives lost.	Americans.
Falaba, March 28, 1915	111	1
Aguila, March 28, 1915	26	..
Gulflight (American), May 1, 1915	3	3
Lusitania, May 7, 1915	1,198	102
Leelanaw (American), July 25	..	..
Iberian, July 31, 1915	6	3
Arabic, August 19, 1915	44	2

SHIPS SUNK AFTER PLEDGE TO UNITED STATES OF SEPTEMBER 1, 1915.

Name. Date.	Lives lost.	Americans.
Hesperian, September 4, 1915	32	..
Ancona, November 7, 1915	206	24
†Persia, December 30, 1915	335	2
Maloja, February 27, 1916	155	..
*Silvius, March 9, 1916	3	..
*Tubania, March 16, 1916	..	..
*Berwindvale, March 16, 1916	..	..
Sussex, March 24, 1916	80	‡
*Manchester Engineer, March 27, 1916	..	..
Zent, April 5, 1916	48	..
Chantala, April 8, 1916	9	..
Santanderino, April 10, 1916	4	..
Rio Branco, May 2, 1916	..	..
Cymric, May 8, 1916	5	..
Mira (French coasting ship), May 16, 1916	§	..
†Batavier V, May 16, 1916	4	1
†Koenigin Wilhelmina, July 31, 1916	3	..
Letimbro, August 2, 1916	x	..
†Kelvina, September 2, 1916	..	..
Marina, October 28, 1916	19	6
Angheliki, October 30, 1916	50	..
Lanao (American), October 28, 1916	..	..
*Arabia, November 6, 1916	2	..
Columbia (American), November 7, 1916	..	..
Chemung (American), November 26, 1916	..	..

*Americans aboard.
†Sunk by mine or torpedo; cause undetermined.
‡Several.
§All on board.
xNumber unknown.

October 8, 1916, German submarine U-53 sunk off Newport, R. I., beyond the 3-mile limit five steamships—the Strathdene, the West Point and Stephano, all British; the Bloomersdijk, Dutch, and the Christian Knudsen, Norwegian. No lives were lost.

Document 4. News clipping from *The Washington Post*, February 1, 1917. [National Archives]

NEW JERSEY DIVISION
NATIONAL WOMAN'S PEACE PARTY

Newark, N.J. March 30, 1917.

Hon. William Branch Wilson,
Secretary of Labor,
Washington, D. C.

Dear Sir:-

The following resolutions passed at a conference of the New Jersey Division of the National Woman's Peace Party, represent the sentiments of a group of earnest, patriotic women. These are the wives, mothers and sisters of men who will be called upon to give their lives in case of war. As such they ask your earnest attention.

We agree with the President's statement that "The example of America must be the example of peace not merely because it will not fight, but of peace because peace is the healing and elevating influence of the world and strife is not," and we stand with him in all his efforts to solve the present crisis by peaceful means.

We, members of the New Jersey Division of the National Woman's Peace Party, hereby reaffirm our expressed belief that war is not a sane or reasonable method of redressing wrong. The fact that American lives have been lost and American property destroyed by warring nations has not altered this conviction.

Document 5a. Letter to Secretary of Labor from National Woman's Peace Party, March 30, 1917. [National Archives]

We believe the only possible justification for our declaring war against Germany at the present time, from the standpoint of those who are asking for war, would be the reasonable hope that such a war would increase the safety of American lives at sea during the present war and during any future war in which Germany might be tempted to violate neutral rights.

Whereas, the probable effect of a declaration of war against Germany would be to increase attacks upon our commerce during this present war, and,

Whereas, a victory by us over her submarines could do no more than secure from her a promise as to her action in a future war, which might or might not be kept, we, therefore, believe that there is a strong probability that after sacrificing thousands of lives, we would find we had not accomplished the one thing that would have justified the war, the present and future safety during war of neutral lives.

We, therefore, respectfully urge that, instead of this method so costly in life and so unsatisfactory in result, the Government of the United States appoint a Joint High Commission to meet representatives of the Imperial German Government, to attempt by joint agreement a settlement of the issues involved. This method has been used with honor by our Government in the past, and we believe, can be used with honor in the present crisis.

Whereas, it is manifest in view of their past history, that however sincere the nations forming the Entente Allies may be in their belief that they are fighting against militarism and for the integrity of the weaker nations, they, nevertheless, have other interests and objects in view growing out of old ambitions and old quarrels.

Document 5b. Letter to Secretary of Labor from National Woman's Peace Party, March 30, 1917. [National Archives]

We, therefore, strongly oppose any alliance which would mean that this nation would give its best life to further ends with which we, as a nation, have no concern.

We would oppose with equal vigor any alliance with Germany were such an alliance in question.

Resolved: That in this as in all future crises, no matter how great the provocation, the question of war or peace be submitted to the people by advisory referendum before Congress declares war.

Whereas, it is possible for the Government to take over for the purpose of national defense the lives of men, it ought also to be possible to take over for these same purposes the property of men.

We demand that upon declaring war now, or at any future time, the Government shall take over all supplies and sources of supplies for our army and navy, compensating for same at cost prices; these prices to be based on salaries paid to workmen in factories, etc., corresponding to salaries paid to officers and soldiers in the army and navy.

It is abhorrent to the best ideals of humanity that it should be to the financial advantage of any individual, firm or corporation to have their fellow men engage in war.

It is abhorrent to us, as wives and mothers, that men should make money out of the death of our husbands and sons.

Earnestly submitted for the New Jersey Division of the National Woman's Peace Party,

(Mrs. Harold S.) *Margaret Stoddard Buttenheim*
State Chairman

Document 5c. Letter to Secretary of Labor from National Woman's Peace Party, March 30, 1917. [National Archives]

Whereas, We as business men and citizens recognize the importance of protecting our property by investing in Fire Insurance, by the employment of an adequate Police Force to protect our property and people. The State assists in this commendable protection, and bringing law breakers to justice, by its admirable and efficient State Constabulary. The State of Pennsylvania also maintains its National Guard, to maimtain peace and surpress riots or invasion. All these powers are used to protect and maintain peace and good order within its borders.

The National or Federal Government, as one of the great family of nations, must depend for its safety and protection on its Army and its Navy. A policeman stationed at a busy street corner of a town or city does not incite to riot, theft or burglary but on the contrary his very presence, will deter persons from such crimes. The State Constabulary does not incite to violations of law, but quite the opposite does deter many, by their presence, from committing offenses. We also know that when it becomes evident to the people of any borough or city that its police force is inadequate, such force is increased, especially upon certain occasions of large gatherings of strangers being within its limits.

Whereas, As we all know that the family of nations of the old world is in trouble and is engaged in a great war, which fact admonishes the United States to follow the advice of a great Statesman, "In time of peace prepare for war", therefore,

Resolved, That this, The Business Men's Association of Towanda, Pennsylvania. request the Hon. Boise   Penrose, the Hon George T. Oliver, our Senators from Pennsylvania, and/the Hon. L. T. McFadden, our representative in Congress, to use all honorable means towards a better preparedness of this nation, by an increase in both Army and Navy.

Attest:

C. M. Finney Secty.

Document 6. Petition of the Business Men's Association of Towanda, PA, December 7, 1915. [National Archives]

State of Rhode Island, &c.

IN GENERAL ASSEMBLY.

January SESSION, A. D. 19 16.

RESOLUTION.

OF THE SENATE OF THE RHODE ISLAND GENERAL ASSEMBLY URGING UPON THE CONGRESS OF THE UNITED STATES OF AMERICA THE DUTY OF ADEQUATELY INCREASING THE MILITARY AND NAVAL FORCES OF THIS GOVERNMENT.

WHEREAS, In view of the terrible loss of human lives and of the ruthless methods that have frequently characterized the present European war, we may realize in some measure the distress and destruction that would be wrought upon our own land should this nation become involved in war with any of the great powers; and

WHEREAS, On several occasions the secretary of state of the United States has made demands that certain fundamental principles of decency and humanity be observed by the participants in this war, demands that this government is notoriously unable to enforce; and

WHEREAS, It is our sacred duty to preserve inviolate this republic with its constitution and traditions of justice, humanity and liberty; now, therefore, be it

RESOLVED, That the honorable senate urges upon the president and congress of the United States the immediate adoption of a definite and continuing policy which shall largely augment our trained and equipped military and naval forces so that this republic may be adequately prepared to resist invasion, to protect the lives and possessions of its citizens, and to enforce its reasonable and humane demands; and also, be it further

RESOLVED, That copies of this resolution be forwarded by the Secretary of State to the members of the Congress of the United States from this State, with instructions to present them in their respective houses.

** ** ** ** ** ** ** ** ** ** **

STATE OF RHODE ISLAND.

OFFICE OF THE SECRETARY OF STATE.

PROVIDENCE.

I HEREBY CERTIFY the foregoing to be a true copy of the original Resolution passed by the Senate of the State of Rhode Island on the 23rd day of February in the year, 1916.

IN TESTIMONY WHEREOF, I have hereunto set my hand and affixed the seal of the State aforesaid this 23rd day of February in the year 1916.

J. Fred Parker

Secretary of State.

Document 7. Resolution of the General Assembly of Rhode Island, February 23, 1916. [National Archives]

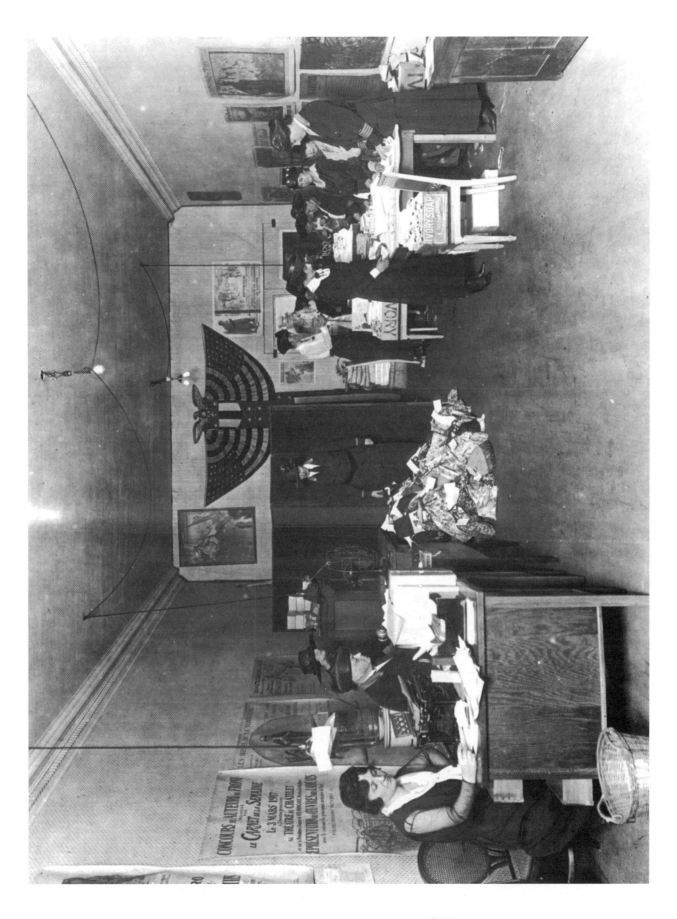

Document 8. Photograph, "Women packing soldiers' comfort kits at the American Overseas Committee," 1918. [National Archives]

Document 9. Photograph, "Members of the 'Women's Land Army' laboring on a farm at Newton Square, Pennsylvania." [National Archives]

Document 10. Photograph, "Female factory office workers volunteering to pack bandages for the American Red Cross," New Britain, CT, February 10, 1919. [National Archives]

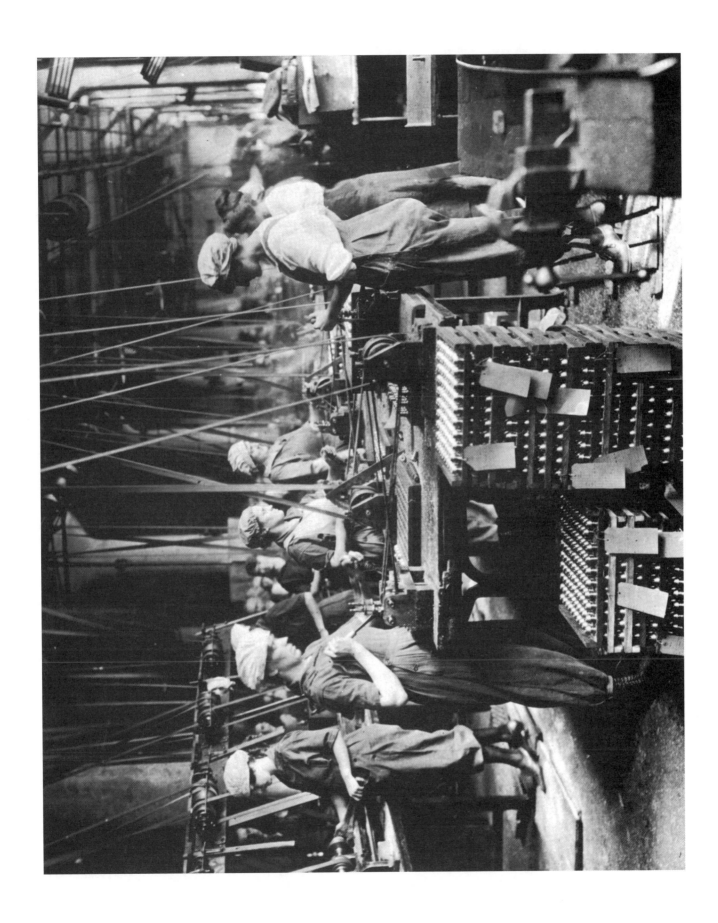

Document 11. Photograph, "Women workers in munitions plant,
Gray & Davis Co.," Cambridge, MA, January 14, 1919. [National Archives]

Document 12. Photograph, "Students at Mt. Holyoke College learning
agricultural duties," South Hadley, MA, August 20, 1918. [National Archives]

Document 13. Photograph, Ordnance Manufacture, n.d. [National Archives]

Document 14. Photograph, "Community Food Demonstration," May 25, 1918. [National Archives]

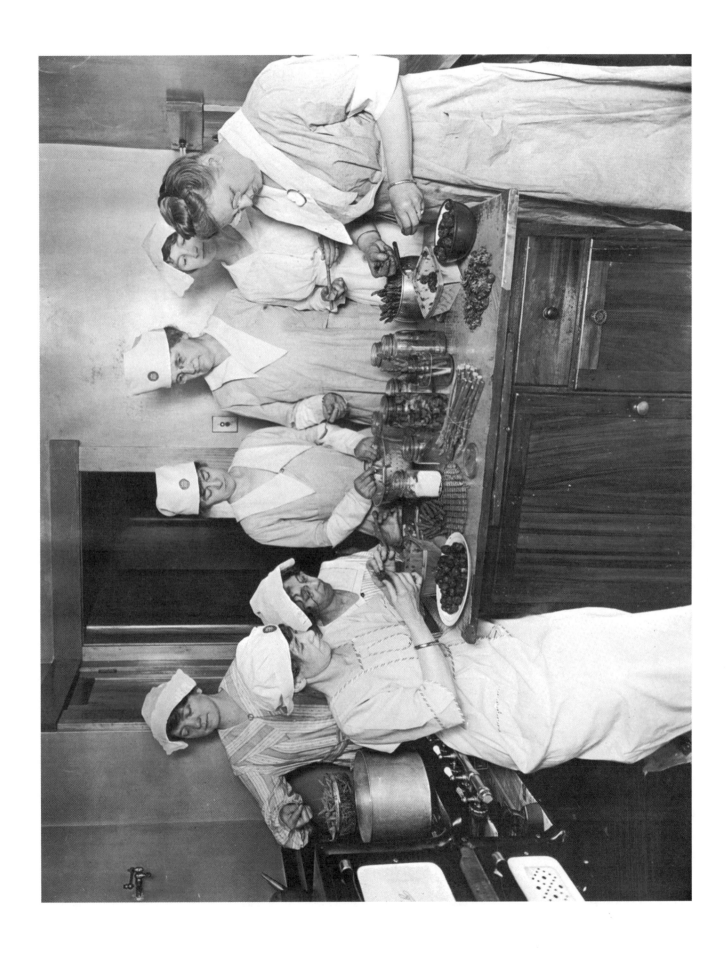

Document 15. Photograph, "Federal Home Demonstration,"
Omaha, NE, June 1918. [National Archives]

DETROIT

CHICAGO

BOSTON

PITTSBURG

ROCHESTER

TRADE MARK.

ACME DIE-CASTING CORPORATION

BUSH TERMINAL, № 5

35TH STREET AND 3RD AVENUE

BROOKLYN, N. Y.

October 23, 1918.

RECEIVED

OCT 24 1918

BUREAU OF WOMEN IN INDUSTRY

Miss Nelle Swartz, Chief,
Bureau of Women in Industry
#230 Fifth Ave.,
New York City.

Dear Madam:-

We are writing this communication in order to place
before you our request that we be permitted at times, say two or
three nights a week, to work some of our hands in the cleaning
department for a few hours overtime.

As Treasurer of the Acme Die Casting Corporation, I
beg to bring the following matters to your attention and for your
consideration.

Our Company manufactures Die Castings, and we are
operating 100% on Government work, principally manufacturing the
Respirators or breathing tube parts for Gas Masks. We have been
requested by the Chemical Warfare Service to speed up production
of their work to the utmost of our ability, as every soldier should
have two Gas Masks, or at least one, in order to protect his life,
and it is well recognized that this is the first requisite which our
men in France require, even though they be twenty miles from the
firing line. On account of this condition and emergency, we have
been working some of our girls overtime on certain days when our casting department crowded the testing department with work.

We might explain that our men in the casting department are
working two shifts, but they do not turn out sufficient to work double
shifts in the testing and clean departments, and so in order to get
out production we have to occassionally work some of our girls overtime to take care of this condition.

One of your Inspectors, Mr. F. Spillman, #230 Fifth Ave.,
New York City called recently and found us violating section 77-4 of
the Labor Laws. We realize that we have violated the law under ex-

Document 16a. Letter to the Bureau of Women in Industry from the
ACME Die-Casting Corporation, October 23, 1918. [National Archives]

tenuating and extreme circumstances. However, we respectfully request a special consideration of our case in view of the above situation, especially as our product is so extremely essential in this national emergency

In view of the Influenza epidemic from which the country at large is now suffering, and from which our plant is similarly effected, we find it more difficult than ever to cope with the situation.

In connection therewith, would it be possible for you to suggest to us some way whereby we do not violate the labor laws, so that we can overcome this occassional accumulation in the testing and cleaning departments. With our present force, and it is difficult to increase same, our schedule of delivery is falling behind and therefore we are looking for some way through which the situation can be relieved. Would it be possible for you to grant us permission to work overtime on certain days, say for about a month or six weeks, which would be helpful.

The above practically presents our case, and you will understand that the Chemical Warfare Service is pressing us very hard for delivery of the die cast metal breathing parts for gas masks, and which are so urgently required for the preservation and protection of the lives of our men fighting abroad.

We understand that this is a matter which will have to be presented to the federal authorities, and will be glad to have as prompt action as possible, so as to avoid our being handicapped in production for any longer time than necessary.

Thanking you for your co-operation in this matter, we remain

Very truly yours,

ACME DIE-CASTING CORPORATION

Treas.

EW/WH

Document 16b. Letter to the Bureau of Women in Industry from the ACME Die-Casting Corporation, October 23, 1918. [National Archives]

Stevens Point, Wis., Aug. 27, 1918.

Wis. State Railway Commission,
Madison, Wis.

Gentlemen:

   I am writing you about a matter of very grave importance to
me as it means my daily bread and butter, and trust you will see it
means much and will consider the question thoroughly.

   I am a widow, absolutely dependent upon my own earnings and
with a "home fire" to keep burning. There are a number of good
positions in this town on the Soo Line, and elsewhere, paying from
sixty-five to eighty dollars per month, which I am perfectly capable
of holding, but, always, I receive the same answer, "You can do the
work, we want to give you the job, but it is an eleven or twelve
hour job, and the present state law says that no woman shall be
employed more than 10 hours per day or to aggregate more than 55
hours per week."

   Now can you tell me how I can hold one of these jobs? How
can I release a man for war work? The law, I appreciate, was
intended primarily as a safeguard to the health of women, but while
this law is still in effect, a woman cannot take but few jobs vacated
by the men. It fairly takes the bread and butter out of the mouth
of the woman wage earner.

   One cannot expect the railways and other companies to put
on three eight-hour shifts, in order to employ women, the expense
would be too great, as each would want a living wage. There are,
right in this town, many young boys from 16 to 20 years of age,
holding down jobs paying from $65 to $80 per month. These boys have
parents, homes; they spend most of their money foolishly; they
waste all the time possible about their work, while women with
homes to keep up, with children or aged parents to support, cannot
take these jobs, which they could fill, and would fill with the
painstaking conscientiousness of a woman, because of this law -
the barrier. They must take so-called "woman's jobs" where they
employ many women at $1.25, $1.50, $1.75, or $2.00 per day, Saturday afternoon off, with the afternoon off always deducted from the
pay check. This state of affairs is not right.

   I can name right now a dozen jobs that I could hold, that
would pay me from $2.75 to $4.50 per day, but the jobs are 11 or 12
hours jobs and they are afraid to give them to me.

   There is one company in this town employing women at work
formerly done by men, running their foundry nine hours per day, but

paying the men for 10 hours work, paying the women who work as long, for nine hours work, on account of this law. They are doing better and faster work than the men did, but receive 32¢ per day less because they cannot be paid for ten hours work, under the law.

It is my belief that a woman can do everything that a man can do that is within her strength. Hundreds and hundreds of women might work and release men for war or war work, could they, the women, be employed on the railroads, etc., in Wisconsin, and work longer than eight hours per day.

Please advise me if any ruling has been made permitting women to work on railroads or do other work necessary to the carrying on of the war. It seems to me such a ruling should be made for the duration of the war; that is, permitting women to work ten or twelve hours shifts, whichever the job required, and guaranteeing them a man's pay for a man's work.

I think this matter is worthy of the consideration of such an august body as the State Railway Commission and I trust you will give my letter the thought which I feel it deserves, and that you will advise me whether or not I can take a job on the railroad here at more than 10 hours per day.

Thanking you, I am

Very truly yours,

(Signed) Mrs. Myrtle Altenburg
743 Michigan Ave.,
Stevens Point, Wis.

Document 17b. Letter to Wisconsin State Railway Commission
from Mrs. Myrtle Altenburg, August 27, 1918. [National Archives]

VALLEY COTTON OIL COMPANY

MEMPHIS, TENN.

October 15, 1918.

Mr. Theodore Hoepfner,
State Factory Inspector,
150 Madison Avenue,
Memphis, Tennessee.

Dear Sir:

We thank you very much for your letter October
14th, giving us the decision of the War Department on the
question of women's working hours.

Inasmuch as, cottonseed oil mills are placed
as we understand it, in priority list as essential industries
from labor, fuel, and supply standpoint, we ask of you to
grant us immediate authority to work our female labor on
twelve hour basis.

We have a most serious emergency at this time, for
our stock of seed is becoming hot and for the past few days the
only labor we have been able to secure to turn seed, and feed
feed to the mill, and unload from cars has been negro women.

As explained to you, in person, however, the women
engaged at an oil mill are not kept continuously at work.
We feel safe in saying that they do not put in over eight
hours in actual work.   And those in the press room not that
much.

We have direct Government contract on lint, contract
number US 3347, and all out output is constmed either as food
or munitions.

In line with your letter we are sending copy of this
letter, in duplicate, to the War Labor Policies Board at
Washington.

Yours truly,

VALLEY COTTON OIL CO.

L. C. Barton,
Manager.

COPY

Document 18. Letter to State Factory inspector from Valley
Cotton Oil Company, October 15, 1918. [National Archives]

U. S. DEPARTMENT OF LABOR
W. B. WILSON, SECRETARY

Issued through
INFORMATION AND EDUCATION SERVICE
Roger W. Babson, Chief

Washington, D. C.

WOMAN IN INDUSTRY SERVICE

This contains a copy of the statement of principles concerning the employment of women in war work as adopted by the War Labor Policies Board. It defines what kind of work women may perform, how they shall best be introduced, under what conditions they should be employed and what work should be prohibited.

Employers should avail themselves of the assistance of the Woman in Industry Service for advice on the best methods of introducing women and the working conditions which should be established.

STANDARDS FOR THE EMPLOYMENT OF WOMEN OUTLINED BY THE WAR LABOR POLICIES BOARD

The War Labor Policies Board, for the Department of Labor, announces the Government's attitude toward the employment of women in war industry. The principles set forth will underlie the work of the Woman in Industry Service, of which Miss Mary Van Kleeck has been appointed Director and Miss Mary Anderson, Assistant Director.

The existing shortage of labor, aggravated daily by the military and naval demands of the Government which requires a greatly increased production of war materials and at the same time the withdrawal from civil occupations of about a quarter of a million additional recruits each month, necessitates widespread recourse to the labor of women in the United States.

In order that their services may be fully utilized and their working power conserved, a clearly defined policy is needed which shall determine what kinds of work women should perform, how they should best be introduced, under what conditions they should be employed, and what work should be prohibited.

Standards as to hours, night work, wages, and conditions of labor have already been defined by the Government in orders issued by the Chief of Ordnance and the Quartermaster General, and in the recommendations made by the War Labor Board, which should be observed by all employers.

First. The shortage of labor in essential war industries should be met in part by further introducing women into occupations easily filled by them, such as clerical and cashier service and accounting in manufacturing, mercantile and financial establishments and in the offices of transportation companies and other public utilities; such as sales clerks and floorwalkers in mercantile establishments, including among others department stores, specialty stores, shoe stores, men's furnishing stores, florists' shops, jewelry stores, drug stores, soda water fountains, etc.

Second.   Women should not be employed to replace men in occupations or places of employment clearly unfit for women owing to the physicial or moral conditions, as for instance, in barrooms and saloons; in pool rooms; in or about mines, smelters, and quarries; on furnace work; in glass works, etc.   In addition, girls under years 21 of age should not be employed in occupations or places of employment clearly unfit for them owing to their youth, as for instance, in the public messenger service, in street car, elevated and subway transportation service, as elevator operators, as bell boys in hotels, and clubs, etc.

Third.   1. The introduction of women into war industries or into employments involving special hazards, such as the use of industrial poisons, should be guided by the standards as to health, comfort and safety set up from time to time by the War Labor Policies Board, in addition to the standards already defined by the Federal Government and by State labor departments.

2. The introduction of women into new occupations such as street railway service, public messenger service, etc., should be guided by regulations concerning hours of labor, night work, etc., such, for instance, as those adopted by the Industrial Commission of Wisconsin for street railway service and by the legislature of New York State for messenger service.

3.   The recruiting of mothers of young children for war industries should be discouraged.

The advice of the Woman in Industry Service should be sought by employers regarding the best methods of introducing women and the working conditions which should be established.

Fourth.   Older men should be more generally employed.   They constitute a largely unused labor reserve.   In the past they have been considered superannuated at early ages. It is estimated that since the war began, the maximum age of engaging men has advanced ten to twelve years, that is, from about 38 to 50.   It has been found that tasks can be graded for these workers according to their strength, and that work unsuitable for women, especially at night, can be performed by them.   In many trades their experience is an asset which offsets less physical strength.   Thus the productive power of this large class now wasted can be utilized.

The needs of the country require the united efforts of all classes of workers, in accordance with their capacities; and to maintain the standards and conditions of labor set up by the Government is, in the words of President Wilson, "indispensable to the Nation's full productive efficiency."

U. S. FOOD ADMINISTRATION

Washington, D. C.

for RELEASE
FOR RELEASE FOR

PAPERS OF JAN .24, 1918.   NO. 81   January 15, 1918.

STATES SECTION
PUBLIC INFORMATION DIVISION

--oOo--

STOP EATING SOLDIERS !

HERBERT KAUFMAN in Cosmopolitan.

If every Cosmopolitan family does its bit, the million house-holds in which this magazine is read can alone save wheat and meat enough to nourish a million fighting men. The need for food con-servation is not "fool conversation." Two sorts of submarines threaten the Allies--the U-boat isn't a whit more effective than the slacker garbage-pail.

If each of you takes care of the little wastes in your home, the big war will soon take care of itself. Women of the United States are the final arbiters of this appalling conflict.

As they write their market-lists, they determine the fate of the state and its foes. Cook the Kaiser's goose on your own stoves.

Victory over there is being weighed upon grocers' scales here.

The flag out front signifies nothing unless it's also hang-ing in the ice-box. Whoever pampers special tastes hampers the army--dines upon the very Stars and Stripes.

We have challenged the dreadest military force in all annals, and we shall fail ignominiously and be marred eternally if our appetites aren't patriots. Stand in the bread-lines of defense--serve ornate and lavish meals now, and you serve the enemy.

Every time you pass the plate for a second helping, Berlin thanks you.

Democracy is equally menaced by gluttony and Germany. Don't crucify Civilization on a cross of knives and forks.

God help a people that stints the field-kitchen to stuff the home larder. It's a shoddy and pinchbeck loyalty that sends sons to the battle-front and won't spare a crust to comrades in arms.

France, England, and Italy can provide as many troops as we'll provision. Extravagant Americans are holding whole regiments from the trenches. Stop eating soldiers!

                    Copyright. By permission of Cosmopolitan.

Document 20b. Press Release No. 81 concerning food conservation, "Stop Eating Soldiers!", January 15, 1918. [National Archives]

The Day's Most Important Messages

From the Government at Washington to the People of the United States

Released by The Committee on Public Information

The Secretary of State   The Secretary of the Navy
The Secretary of War   George Creel

German agents are spreading poisonous stories that accuse American officers of having immoral relations with Red Cross nurses in France. It has even been circumstantially reported, in all parts of the country, that 200 nurses were returned recently from France in a state of pregnancy. Because of these stories the Red Cross authorities are finding it difficult to obtain nurses for service abroad. Parents are refusing to allow their daughters to go. The stories are without foundation. They are entirely the work of German propagandists. The nurses in France work under the very best conditions and there has not been a suspicion against any of them. The story of the return of 200 is ridiculously false.

On account of reports of overcrowding in Washington, fifty per cent of the eligible clerks on the civil service list have been refusing to come to the capital to work, and government departments are consequently handicapped. It is true that in Washington hotel rooms and furnished apartments and small houses are hard to find, but there are plenty of rooms such as war workers need. Enough have been inspected and listed to take care of applicants for three months to come. Prices are moderate. The District Council of Defence is seeing to that.

It is not true that the planting of winter wheat has been "discouraged by price-fixing." The farmers have planted forty-two million acres of winter wheat. That is two million acres more than ever before and seven million acres more than the average acreage before the war. It is estimated that the yield will be 122,000,000 bushels more than last year.

It is not true that the Food Administration has fixed the price of tomatoes. It has merely sent out to tomato growers an announcement that the army and navy were ready to receive tenders for canned tomatoes based on a stated price per ton for raw tomatoes. No canner was required to bid and no limit was set on the price that he might ask.

The Food Administration has fixed the price of no farm product except wheat. The price and supply of wheat had to be protected because the allied governments had set single agencies to buy food stuffs in America, and their purchases of wheat were sufficient to control our prices and drain off our supplies unless the authorities at Washington intervened to save our people from famine prices and a shortage of wheat.

Newspaper despatches have accused the Ordnance Bureau of delaying the manufacture of big guns in this country by an attempt to improve on the recoil mechanisms of the famous French 75's. The report is a falsehood. There had never been any machinery built in America to work so accurately on so large a scale as is necessary for the production of these recoil mechanisms. They must not be "off" two one-thousandths of an inch in a distance of more than six feet. The Ordnance Department had to persuade manufacturers to undertake this difficult work and to assist them financially in the building of a 13 acre plant and in the purchase and manufacture of six million dollars' worth of special tools. The plant is now completed and is turning out the mechanisms. The delay was inherent in the difficulties that had to be overcome. It was not due to any attempt to improve on a recoil mechanism that is the secret of the superiority of the best heavy gun on the European battlefields.

Contributions to the American work of reconstruction in France are being discouraged by means of reports that the reconstructed villages are likely to be retaken by the Germans. These reports are circulated by German agents. They are untrue. The villages that are being rebuilt are far behind the fighting zone and the work of reconstruction is chiefly devoted to procuring tractors and farm implements and to reclaiming fields for cultivation.

There were many complaints last winter, that the price-fixing order of the Fuel Administration had led to the output of a bituminous coal full of slate and other impurities. The Fuel Administrator has organized an inspection system to overcome this condition. Coal condemned will be sold for fifty cents a ton less than the fixed price for the mine.

In spite of all denials, stories continue to circulate charging our soldiers in France with wholesale immorality and consequent disease. When the draft army was assembled in our cantonments 400 out of every 1000 men were admitted to the hospitals to be treated for venereal diseases. The rate for the National Army is now 69.8 per thousand. For the regular army it is 69.2. For the expeditionary forces in France it is as low as 51.7 per thousand. Military training and discipline have improved the health of the men in this regard as in all others.

Ways to *do something* for *your Country!*

A few suggestions

Courtesy of U. S. Food Administration

Paul Stahr

THE Committee on Public Information, 10 Jackson Place, Washington, D. C., has issued a splendid pamphlet entitled "National Service Handbook" which enumerates the various ways that men and women can "do something" to help. We strongly recommend that all who want to "do something" should write for it. (15c.)

In the following classification we have not included any of the many different kinds of Military Service and Government work for which men and women are greatly needed. The following is a list of things that can be done, in addition to giving money to war charities, by people who have to remain in civilian life:

What Everyone should do

1. **Buy War Saving Stamps.** No one is too poor to buy thrift stamps and W. S. S. **Save for Liberty Loans** and buy bonds during the campaigns. Without **your** money the war cannot be won.

2. **Eat wisely.** Eat what is plentiful. Save wheat, meat, sugar and fats. Waste nothing. Join the U. S. Food Administration, Washington, D. C. Write for a pledge card.

3. **Support the President** and the Government in all that they are doing to conduct the war efficiently. Knocking does not do any good. If you knew the difficulties of the task of carrying on a war, you would realize that the Government has been doing exceedingly well.

4. **Give our soldiers and sailors a good time.** If you live near a military camp, invite them to your home for meals. If you do not know any of them, apply to the commanding officer for names of particularly homesick ones.

5. **Read about and understand the war.** Keep informed as to what our country is doing. Read the newspapers and the weekly magazines. Roosevelt said: "It is the duty of every citizen to inform himself on the war."

6. **Oppose premature peace talk**—for a German peace now will mean another war in a few years.

7. **Report any disloyalty** to the United States to the Department of Justice, Washington, D. C. Also report the name of any one spreading German propaganda or war rumors you think to be untrue and harmful.

What You can do with part of your time

1. **The American Red Cross** and other war charities are anxious to get volunteer workers for office work, rolling bandages, making trench candles, etc.

2. **Knit sweaters, mufflers and helmets** for the Red Cross. Apply for directions at local headquarters.

3. Join the **War Emergency Section.** See below.

4. If you can do platform speaking, apply to the **Four Minute Men,** 10 Jackson Place, Washington, D. C., for information and address of nearest headquarters.

5. **Do Americanization work.** Help teach immigrants English. Apply to your local Dep't of Education.

6. **Preserve vegetables and fruits** when they are plentiful.

7. **Plant and grow** as much foodstuffs as possible. Apply to the United States Department of Agriculture, Washington, D. C. for special instructions.

What You can do with all of your time

1. Join the **U. S. Public Service Reserve,** 1712 Eye St., Washington, D. C. This branch of the U. S. Department of Labor is recruiting executives, professional men, skilled workmen for various government departments. Write for an application blank. Membership is only open to men and does not absolutely bind one to service.

2. Join the **War Emergency Section,** Department of Labor, Washington, D. C. This organization is doing for women what the U. S. Public Service Reserve is doing for men.

3. Apply to the **U. S. Civil Service Commission,** Washington, D. C. for government stenographic and clerical positions.

4. The **U. S. Boys' Working Reserve,** 1712 Eye St., Washington, D.C., is enrolling boys between the ages of 16 and 21 for work on farms and in war industries during the summer vacation.

This list is not by any means complete. Do something to help. That is the important thing. "Remember that your first duty is to your country and that you will find your highest personal success in public service."

National Committee of Patriotic Societies

Southern Building, Washington, D. C.

For Release in afternoon newspapers at the convenience of the Editor.
(From the Committee on Public Information, Washington, D.C.)

Note to the Editor:- This service is released by the Committee to expose new specific instances of German propaganda in this country. These denials are from official
sources and may be regarded as authoritative.

THE DAILY GERMAN LIE

By Harvey O'Higgins, Associate Chairman,
Committee on Public Information.

    In the neighborhood of all shipbuilding plants, German sympathizers have
been spreading stories of accidents and deaths among the workmen. The stories
are untrue. The Shipping Board reports that the casualties in the shipyards
are much below those in other similar industries. From the beginning of our
shipbuilding campaign, precautions have been taken to safeguard the workers.
Shipping Board investigators regularly visit all plants. They not only investigate safety precautions, but medical and hospital facilities, sanitation,
housing, transportation, food, and even recreation for the men. They see that
sewers are built, swamps are drained, houses are kept sanitary, food supplies
are good, and the health and comfort of the men in every way protected. The
government is taking the same sort of care of shipyard workers that it took of
the men engaged in building the Panama Canal.

    Similar falsehoods are told to discourage loyal citizens from enrolling
for government war work. They are assured that it is "just like enlisting";
that the government holds all men who enroll and orders them from place to
place; that whites and negroes are fed and housed together, and so forth.
These untruths are being successfully exposed and contradicted by the newspapers in many localities.

--------O--------

    The campaign against the Red Cross having failed, the pro-Germans are now
busy with slanders against the Y.M.C.A. That association supplies free to the
soldiers moving picture entertainments, lectures, concerts, stationery,
athletic equipment, library equipment, etc. It has been selling cigarettes
and tobacco to the soldiers at cost. The cost to the association has been
higher than the price at which the army canteens could sell the same goods,
because the army does not have to pay freight and transportation charges. The
Y.M.C.A. is now selling "smokes" at the same price as the Quartermaster's
stores, and meeting the deficit out of the general funds of the association.
It is estimated that the deficit will amount to two million dollars a year, at
least.

    Meanwhile, the pro-Germans have been circulating all manner of stories
charging graft and profiteering among the Y.M.C.A. workers in France. A
thorough investigation has been made without finding any ground for those
charges. The association is giving a much needed service in France and doing
it patriotically. All its operations are under the eye of the military authorities, and if there were any such abuses as the pro-Germans allege the army
officers would report them promptly for correction.

--------O--------

    A correspondent in Mount Holly, N. C., furnishes a pro-German story to
the effect that President Wilson had been invited to address the convention of
a fraternal order, "that this invitation was not acknowledged and that the
President did not attend the meeting, but some delegates on their way home
stopped in Washington and made inquiry and were advised that Mr. Wilson had not
received the invitation, the inference being that Mr. Tumulty withheld the invitation from the President."

The story is a baseless lie. It is part of the pro-German campaign to take advantage of religious differences in this country, arouse anti-Catholic, anti-Protestant and anti-Hebrew prejudices, and set us fighting each other instead of fighting Germany.

****

German propagandists both here and in Germany are announcing that in a recent damage suit arising out of the loss of the Lusitania, it was proved before the court and admitted by the judge that the steamship was an armed munitions boat carrying explosives. As a matter of fact the suit was heard by Judge Julius M. Mayer of the Admiralty branch of the United States district court in New York, and Judge Mayer declared in his findings that it had been proved beyond all doubt that the Lusitania was not armed, and never had been armed, and carried no explosives on the voyage on which she was torpedoed and sunk.

****

The recent reverses in France seem to have affected the workmanship of the inventors of anti-American pro-German slanders. Many of their falsehoods are too ridiculous to be worth contradicting. In Minnesota, they are passing around word that any woman who marries a U. S. soldier will be put in prison by the government. In Kansas, farmers are being told that "everyone who has more than a bushel of potatoes on the first of September will have to give them to the Red Cross or to the government officials." Santa Rosa, Cal., hears that "numerous highly paid government clerks and employees of the Protestant faith have been removed in order that their positions might be taken by Catholics." Huntington, Indiana, has had the story that at Camp Shelby "they are importing negro girls of thirteen and fourteen years old" for the troops— a slander which the Huntington Herald promptly investigated and disproved. Other localities report similar short-term lies, so soon discounted or so easily disproved that it would seem the originators of them are losing their cunning.

****

A hotel guest at Asbury Park, N. J., has heard the following story from a chance acquaintance, who declared he had been told it by an eye-witness.

"While travelling on a ferry from New York City, he noticed a young man and woman standing at one end of the boat. The woman was wrapped in a large blue cloak. At intervals, the man would take out his handkerchief and wipe the lips of the woman, who seemed to be dribbling at the mouth. The people began to gather around the couple, and the man becoming humiliated drew the cloak from the woman, who turned out to be armless and whose tongue had been cut out. Later it developed that the young woman was just returning from France where she had been on duty as a Red Cross nurse."

Stories of this sort have been put in circulation in all parts of the country since the call went out for Red Cross volunteers for service in France. All the stories that were precise enough to be investigated have been found to be false. No mutilated American nurse has been returned to this country and none has been reported in France. The reports seem obviously designed to discourage nurses from volunteering.

The correspondent who reports the picturesque lie from Asbury Park unfortunately did not ask the name of his "chance acquaintance" or inquire who was the "eye witness" who had vouched for the yarn. Loyal citizens are asked to obtain correct names and addresses in all such cases and send the information to the Department of Justice, Washington, D. C.

****

In parts of the South, a very circumstantial account is being reported of how Madame Schumann-Heink, arrested as a German spy, had committed suicide. Many inquiries as to the truth of the report have come to the Committee on Public Information. There is, of course, no truth whatever in it. Madame Schumann-Heink has been aggressive in her loyal Americanism, and the Kaiserites are apparently attempting to discredit her by circulating this slander, out of revenge. They spread it in the South, because she has been publicly active in support of war charities etc. further north, and any report of her suicide would be somewhat discredited by her subsequent appearance on the concert stage.

****

Document 24. Poster, "Beat Back the Hun with Liberty Bonds," Third Liberty Loan, n.d. [National Archives]

FOOD WILL WIN THE WAR
You came here seeking Freedom
You must now help to preserve it
WHEAT is needed for the allies
Waste nothing

Document 25. Poster, "Food Will Win the War," Food Administration, n.d. [National Archives]

Document 26. Poster, "Sure! We'll Finish the Job," Victory Liberty Loan, n.d. [National Archives]

Document 27. Poster, "Team Work Wins," Food Administration, n.d. [National Archives]

4

Hot Springs 18th February. 1918

Sir.

I was born in Germany, City of Berlin 1883. I left that Country in 1899. for the United States, there I stayed about 6 months in N.Y. and went then to Australia, wich I left about 6 months before the outbreak of the European war, and reached the Phill ippines where I paid my taxes and followed my proffession wich is that of a Mechanic and Chauffeur I have never been interned nor put under any kind of restraint, because my opinion about the war was known and my loyalty to the Cause of the Al lies never doubted, but things got bad over there in my line of work, and as at that time some German interned Prisoners was to be send over here on the U.S. a Transport Sherman I made an application to the Phillipp. Constabulary for Trans portation on that Transport wich they Granted

Document 28a. Letter from C. Ludwig Schonberg to Acting Director of Internment, February 18, 1918. [National Archives]

me with the assurance that I would not be inter
ned over here, but wich I am, and for wich I donot
see any neccensity. Sir I left Germany at the age
of 16. have never served the German army nor
intend doing so. I lost my Nationality First =
By not returning when of Military age
Second = By staying away from that Country
over 10 years. Third = Because I did not e
ven at the outbreak of the war report by a ger
man Consul for Military Service, I have nothing
in common with, it. Sir I am all day long com
pelled to stay here among a lot of People wich
have nothing in common with me, and wich
knowing my Political Ideas donot in any way
make my stay here pleasant. Naturally I up
hold the Cause of the Allies, and since I have
been a boy, I have lived among them and worked
for them and earned my daily bread of them

Document 28b. Letter from C. Ludwig Schonberg to Acting
Director of Internment, February 18, 1918. [National Archives]

I am sure I have some reason to uphold there Cause rather then the land though I have been born there jet from wich I never received any benefit worsthall. Sir I am all alone here amoings a set of people that make me absolutely miserable, therefore I make the above humble petition, and being in that position I am sure You can Picture in Your mind what a great joy it would be to me to be set free from the loathsome company in wich I am compelled to stay. If the Chance were given me to join the U. S. A. or any other branch in the Service of U. S. I am sure I would proove by faithfull Service my Gratitude, to a people wich I reverence, and of wich I would like to have the honor in the future to be one. Sir I am absolutely helpless and friendless in this matter. Sir but still hoping to get a favorable answer to this my humble Petition Sir I am sure should You be so just and kind

4

and grant my reasonable Petition, I swear You shall never regret the day that You have granted me the same, for I shall always in word and in deed prove my loyalty both to You and to the old U.S.A.

Thanking You in anticipation I remain, Yours always Gratefully

C. Ludwig Schonberg

MAX EASTMAN, Editor   FLOYD DELL, Managing Editor   MERRILL ROGERS, Business Manager

The MASSES

34 Union Square, East
NEW YORK

This Magazine is owned and Published Cooperatively by its Editors. It has no Dividends to Pay, and nobody is trying to make Money out of it. A Revolutionary and not a Reform Magazine; a Magazine with a Sense of Humor and no Respect for the Respectable; Frank; Arrogant; Impertinent; Searching for the True Causes; a Magazine Directed against Rigidity and Dogma wherever it is found; Printing what is too Naked or True for a Money-Making Press; a Magazine whose final Policy is to do as it Pleases and Conciliate nobody, not even its Readers——A Free Magazine

Dear Friend:

The war has come in spite of our efforts. Military expediency and patriotic emotionalism will now dominate the organs of public opinion.

This is to tell you that one magazine is going to fight militarization, and fight nationalistic prejudice, 'and think clearly and try to tell the truth without patriotic sentimentality and without patriotic hatred.

It is going to fight conscription.

It is going to fight the censorship.

It is going to stand up against those forces of industrial privilege that will seize the occasion of this war to Prussianize America.

It is going to fight The Iron Heel.

I don't know whether any other magazines will do this or not but I know they will be few in number.

To keep light shining out of the ideas that are true and enduring throughout this storm of black passions -- that is the task of a few of us.

Will you help?

It is going to require money to sustain THE MASSES through this crisis.

Will you send us $3.00 and the names of two people who will read a magazine that tries to tell the truth and advocate human liberty even in war time?

If you can send more than $3.00 and more than two names, do it.

We must make the people know what war means. We face the menace of a militarized America.

Yours sincerely,

Max Eastman

Editor.

ME:JAE
BS&AU-12646

Document 29. Letter from Max Eastman, editor of the magazine, *The Masses*, to the public, n.d. [National Archives]

McGregor Ia.
Apr 8- 1918

Hon Mr Haugen
    Dear Sir
As the air is ringing
with Americanism, I for
one would like to see the
German Language prohibited
in America. I live in a
German settlement and the
young children cannot
understand the english
language until they go
to school. how can we
know how the Germans
may be plotting against
us when we cannot
understand their language.
if they want to live in
America why not pass a
law that they should
use our language.
    Yours Resp.
        E.E. Brewer.

E.B.B. -

16246

Department of Justice
—
United States Attorney's Office

New York

G

Nov'r 30 1917

9-12-9-36-0

The Attorney General,

Washington, D. C.

RECORDS

S i r :

I beg to enclose copy of a new indictment against the Masses Publishing Company,
Max Eastman, and others, which was filed on the
26th of November, 1917, superseding the indictment filed November 19th, a copy of which was
recently sent you.

The new indictment charges the making
of the conspiracy subsequent to the 15th day of
June, 1917, whereas the former indictment charged
it as being made subsequent to the 6th day of
April, 1917; otherwise the indictments are identical.

The prosecution in this case is based upon
certain articles and cartoons appearing in "The
Masses" for August, September and October, 1917.
I believe that it will be possible to satisfy the
jury that the objectionable articles and cartoons
were published with the specific intent of obstruct-
ing recruiting and enlistment, and of promoting

Document 31a. Letter from United States Attorney's Office, New York, to Attorney General,
Washington, DC, concerning Max Eastman, November 30, 1917. [National Archives]

disloyalty in the enlisted forces.

    For the purpose of showing this specific
intent I intend to introduce in evidence, if
possible, an article written by Max Eastman, and
published in the June 1917 issue of "The Masses".
This article contains the following quotation:-

> "We wish to persuade those who
> love liberty and democracy enough to give
> their energy or their money or their
> lives for it, to withhold the gift from
> this war, and save it to use in the sad
> renewal of the real struggle for liberty
> that will come after it.   We want them
> to resist the war-fever and the patriotic
> delirium, the sentimental vanity, the
> sentimental hatred, the solemn hypocrisies
> of idealists, resist the ceremonious in-
> stallations of petty tyranny in every
> department of our lives, _resist conscrip-
> tion if they have the courage_, and at
> whatever cost to their social complaisance
> save themselves for a struggle of human
> liberty against oppression that will be
> what it says it is." (Italics mine)

    The June issue of "The Masses" from which
the above extract is taken was printed and distributed
about May 10th of this year.   That, of course, was
before the Conscription or Selective Draft Act became
a law, but, according to my information, at a date when
the bill had passed both Houses of Congress and was
in conference.

A question of law will arise at the
trial as to whether a statement of the policy of
the magazine made prior to the enactment of the
Conscription Law may be introduced as evidence of
the intention of the publication subsequent to the
enactment of the law.   I would be very glad if
you will send me any authorities on this point that
you may have in your files.

It will be necessary also to prove the
status of the Conscription Bill on the date that the
June issue was published.   Will you be good enough
to let me know who would be in a position to give
testimony on this point at the trial of these
defendants?

Respectfully,

[signature: Warren G. Coffey]

U. S. Attorney.

Incl. 15579

ALBERT D. LEYHE
ATTORNEY AND COUNSELLOR AT LAW
207-208 NATIONAL BANK OF ARIZONA BLDG.
PHOENIX. ARIZONA

December,
fifth,
1 9 1 8,

Department of Justice,
Washington, D. C.

My dear Sir:-

In June, 1917, 35 young men, subjects of Russia, residing in
the Salt River Valley, Arizona, were arrested for failure to register under the United States Selective Draft law, and In August
of the same year they were given trial, and sentenced to one year
in the County jail at Prescott, Arizona, which sentence they served.
During the period of their confinement, however, questionairs were
handed each of them, and were signed by all of the 34 that were im-
prisoned (one of them having been seriously ill was not in prison)
except six of the number who refused to sign same, and for such re-
fusal said six of their number were, at the expiration of the term
of service, rearrested for refusual to sign questionairs, and were
sent to Ft. Huachuca, Arizona, and later four of them found their
way to Ft. Leavensworth, Kansas, and two of them were, at the last
account, held in the guard house at Ft. Riley.

These people as you are aware are of a religious organization
founded in Russia, more than 300 years ago, and which has for one of
its definite creeds, a settled conviction against war, or the engagment
in it by any of the members of the organization. I understand that
the ancestors of some of these men who are now confined at the Forts
above named, have suffered, in Russia, injuries, tortures, and even death,
rather than give up their religious convictions. They came to America
where they hoped to find a place where they could worship God according to the dicates of their own conscience, and while we who are native
born and have been reared - under American influences, do not agree
with these people in their religious doctrines, and while our convictions is that the welfare of our Country and the protection of our homes,
should be first in our thoughts, yet impartial judgment must give
to these people credit for the zeal with which they adhere to their
accepted beliefs.

It seems that those now confined are all related in some way
by blood or marriage, and a number of other of their relatives live
in this valley, and they have concluded they should like to seek other
places where they might gather, and live more secluded to themselves,
and where they might have in a measure the making of laws which should
govern them, and have asked me to convey to you a request that the six
members now confined at the above-named Forts be released so that the
whole number could sojourn otherwheres. They ask this at this time
because of the termination of the War in which their services were requested, and because the men confined have already served about a year
and four months imprisonment, as a punishment for their disobedience of
our laws. I shall be glad to have you wire me whether you would take
kindly to their suggestion. Thanking you in advance for your immediate
communication in response.

Very truly yours,

Document 32. Letter from A. D. Leyhe to Justice Department, December 5, 1918. [National Archives]

9-5-142

NEW YORK CABLE ADDRESS "WALDORF, NEW YORK."
PHILADELPHIA CABLE ADDRESS "BELLEVUE, PHILADELF

THE WALDORF

THE BELLEVUE-STRATFORD

THE ASTORIA

THE WALDORF-ASTORIA, NEW YORK.
THE BELLEVUE-STRATFORD, PHILADELPHIA.

The Waldorf-Astoria,

New York, Sept. 25th 1918

DEPARTMENT OF JUSTICE
SEP 1918
MAILS AND FI...

RECORDED 9-5-142-35

Hon. Thos. W. Gregory atty gen
Washington D.C.

Dear Sir: I Enclose clipping giving an account of the activities last week of Rose Pastor Stokes.

As she is advocating the things for which Debs was convicted, she should be arrested and brought to trial again if there is going to be any delay in beginning to serve her sentence. This is no time to allow her to abuse the courts and oppose our war program. She should be suppressed at once.

Yours truly
W. J. Payne — Richmond Va

ROSE STOKES ASSAILS JURY.

Says "Triers" of Debs Had "Ears Stuffed by Stocks and Bonds."

Speaking before a gathering of several thousand Socialists at Beethoven Hall, Fifth Street and Third Avenue, yesterday, Rose Pastor Stokes, who is under a sentence of ten years' imprisonment for seditious speech, described her impressions of the trial of Eugene Debs, former Socialist candidate for President, who was recently convicted in Cleveland of a crime similar to that charged against Mrs. Stokes. Both defendants are out on bail pending the determination of appeals that have been taken to the higher courts.

According to Mrs. Stokes, Debs was tried by a jury composed of men incapable of understanding who he was and the ideas for which he stood.

"It looked to me," she said, "as though most of them had gone to sleep before the civil war, or at least had never been awakened since that time. The only slaves they knew of were the colored slaves of the civil war, and having freed those slaves, they had no appreciation of the fact that industrial development in this country had produced another slave—the wage slave, for whose freedom Debs was fighting as ardently as Lincoln ever fought for the freedom of the colored slave.

"Yet, before such men—old men, with eyes blinded by securities, and ears stuffed by stocks and bonds, was Eugene Debs tried and convicted. How could the result be otherwise?"

Mrs. Stokes gave a description of the courtroom in which Debs was tried, referring to the judge as a "man who rocked back and forth in his chair and only needed some knitting in his hands to complete the picture.

Document 34. Newspaper clipping concerning speech made by Rose Pastor Stokes, September 25, 1918. [National Archives]

LAW OFFICES
OF
LAZARUS S. DAVIDOW
726-728 PENOBSCOT BUILDING
CHERRY 6084
DETROIT, MICHIGAN
118

9-5-142

9-5-142-36

OCT 11 18

September 18th., 1918.

Hon. Woodrow Wilson,
 President of the United States of America,
Washington, D.C.
My dear Mr. Wilson:

On Sunday, September 15th.,1918, in the city of Detroit, state of Michigan, Rose Pastor Stokes delivered a lecture in the House of the Masses, a hall rented for the purpose of hearing Mrs. Stokes speak. This meeting was attended by several representatives of the Department of Justice who stayed thru-out the lecture and who made no effort at any time to interrupt the speaker.

In the midst of her talk, several representatives of the Detroit Police Department and the American Protective League entered this hall which was crowded with men,women and children. They compelled the speaker to stop and forced all the men in the audience to pass out of the hall into an adjoining room where they were made to exhibit their registration and classification cards. When the men had filed in again, after having been made acquainted with this form of terroism (which, if we are to believe the recent newspaper reports, is not peculiar to Detroit) the lecturer went on with her talk and concluded it without any further interruptions.

I shall not mention to you the various indignities to which the men were subjected. I am merely calling to your attention the fact that first, these officious zealots tried to break up a peaceful assembly and secondly, that the men attending this lecture were herded together like cattle and subjected to individual quizzes by those who, while they were American Protective League operatives and policemen, certainly had no authority to compel such an outrage.

Nowhere in the "Draft Act" do I find any provision that permits men to be stopped and to be compelled to show their registration cards. Nowhere do I find any provision that grants any authority to the Police or others to interrupt peaceful assemblies. If a man is accused or suspected of having failed to comply with the "Draft Act" in the matter of registration, he may be arrested only upon a warrant having first been issued for his arrest by the proper authorities. If it is necessary that our civil rights be suspended because these times demand their suspension, then I submit, Mr. President, that a law ought to be passed or the Constitution be amended to that effect, so that by legal process and not by acts of despotism and tyrany shall slackers be taken into custody and disposed of. I feel that the usurpation of authority in the manner I have described will have but one effect, and that is a growing disrespect on the part of the people for law and order; because, if the so-called authorities may take the law into their own hands, pray why not the ordinary man ?

In these days when we are being called upon to make the utmost sacrifices so that the world may be made safe for Democracy, it comes with little grace that men on the plea of Patriotism should flagrantly violate the rights which are secured us by the Constitution and for the preservation of which we have entered the gigantic struggle across the sea. I know, Mr. President, that there are legal remedies for the correction of the wrong above mentioned. But I feel that resorting to legal process will not be as efficacious as a public statement from you.

(1)

Document 35a. Letter from Lazarus Davidow to President Wilson, September 18, 1918. [National Archives]

Hon. Woodrow Wilson, (continued)

You have previously given utterance of your position regarding acts of lawlessness which are perpretrated in the name of patriotism. The incident I have narrated to you is not local to Detroit, but prevalent thruout the entire country, and I feel quite sure that this is a time and a situation which requires another public expression from you, which will put a stop to this species of lawlessness, whether it consists of lynching or the terroism above described.

      Awaiting your reply, I am

          Sincerely yours,

Document 35b. Letter from Lazarus Davidow to President Wilson, September 18, 1918. [National Archives]

Sparta, Ga.,
Nov. 5, 1917.

Hon. Mr. Wilson,
Secretary of Labor,
Washington, D.C.

9/10ᵛ

Dear Sir:

As labor will play a most important part in this world war for democracy I want to call your attention to the value of colored labor in this great struggle. The colored man has come forth at the call of the government offering his life in the defense of the colors without hesitation and will give the last full measure of devotion this country in the trenches and the various fields of labor. All he asks is a chance to do his bit. He is proud of the chance the government has

Document 36a. Letter from Charles B. Johnson to
Secretary of Labor, November 5, 1917. [National Archives]

thus far given him. According to newspaper reports the government and great industrial plants need laborers, in the mines and other places, skilled and unskilled. In various sections of the south there is a surplus of laborers. They do not read the papers and don't know where work can be found. The colored laborer is the most loyal and dependable in America at this critical time. If he was equally distributed over the country where needed, it would wonderfully help the labor question. He is no striker — but a worker. In this struggle the government does not need strikers but loyal workers.

I want to humbly suggest to you the idea being followed by other departments in giving the

Document 36b. Letter from Charles B. Johnson to Secretary of Labor, November 5, 1917. [National Archives]

colored labor representation among your advisers, through whom the colored laborer could appeal to the Labor Department for protection and before whom present his grievances. A government labor agent among our people who do not read newspapers would be of great value to them and the government in the way of information. A colored man on your staff of advisers would greatly stimulate colored labor.

I am a college graduate and have done post-graduate work at Columbia University, New York City, and have taught in three states for twenty years and am widely known. I shall be glad to render you my service in whatever capacity needed in the Labor Department.

Document 36c. Letter from Charles B. Johnson to Secretary of Labor, November 5, 1917. [National Archives]

We as a race loyal to a fault shall appreciate your giving us recognition and a chance. The world does not know the value of colored labor. Ignorance and oppressive laws have kept him down. Let him rise. He is needed. We shall be glad to have representation in your department similar to Mr. Scott in the War Department. Pardon me for the liberty thus taken. I am only interested in the world war and my race.

Yours truly,
Chas B. Johnson.

International Longshoremens Ass'n
Local No. 306, Hoboken, N. J.

Affiliated with AMERICAN FEDERATION OF LABOR

PRESIDENT	SECRETARY
....	....
ADDRESS	ADDRESS
....	....

Hoboken, N. J., ——July 28,———— 191 7.

Hon. W. B. Wilson,

      Secretary of Labor,

           Washington, D. C.

Dear Sir::

      Complying with your instruction of July 25th, I am sending you a list of names, all members of the International Longshoremen's Association, who have been discharged or are not permitted to work on account of German extraction on the Hoboken Piers. The undersigned has personally collected the names, and wishes to say that statements hereto attached are truthful in every respect. Furthermore, up to this time I could not secure more names, but am ready to get more, if necessary, as time has been limited to get a larger list.

      Hoping you will at your earliest convenience adjust the unpleasant matter, I remain

                  Yours respectfully,

                      John Gunlach

                    Secretary Local 306 I. L. A.

International Longshoremens Ass'n
Local No. 306, Hoboken, N. J.

Affiliated with AMERICAN FEDERATION OF LABOR

PRESIDENT	SECRETARY
ADDRESS	ADDRESS

Hoboken, N. J., _____ *191*

LIST OF NAMES.

----

1. PAUL SPRINGER: Married; working 18 years as Longshoreman. Has first paper one year. Discharged on account of German extraction.

2. WILLIAM REUTENKRANZ: Married; working 16 years as Longshore-man. Is a citizen since 1906. Discharged on account of German extraction.

3 FREDERIK SCHUSSLER: Working 10 years as Longshoreman. Is a citizen since 1913. Discharged on account of German ex-traction.

4. PAUL SPARMAN: Married; working 17 years as Longshoreman. Is a citizen since 1911. Discharged on account of German extraction.

5. LUDWIG BURMEISTER: Working 20 years as Longshoreman. Is a citizen since 1901. Discharged on account of German ex-traction.

6. JOHN GUNLACH: Married. Working 12 years as Longshoreman. Is a citizen since 1913. Not permitted to work on ac-count of German extraction.

Document 37b. Letter from John Gunlach to Honorable
W. B. Wilson, July 28, 1917. [National Archives]

International Longshoremens Ass'n
Local No. 306, Hoboken, N. J.

Affiliated with AMERICAN FEDERATION OF LABOR

PRESIDENT	SECRETARY
....	....
ADDRESS	ADDRESS
....	....

2,   *Hoboken, N. J.,* ————————— *191*

7. WILLIAM GALTEN: Married; working 8 years as Longshoreman.
    Has first paper four years. Discharged on account of
    German extraction.

8. GEORGE JOHN CORNILS: Married; working 20 years as Longshore-
    man. Is a citizen since 1898.
    George John Cornils, Jr., drafted. Not permitted to
    work on account of German extraction.

9. CHRISTIAN DAMAN. Married; working 20 years as Longshoreman.
    Is a citizen since 1894. Not permitted to work on ac-
    count of German extraction.

10. HENRY BEHNKE: Working 5 years as Longshoreman. Has first
    paper four years. Not permitted to work on account of
    German extraction.

11. JOHN LUTH: Married; working 12 years as Longshoreman. Is a
    citizen since 1912; also in the first draft, No. 353.
    Discharged on account of German extraction.

12. FERDINAND SANKOWSKY: Working 17 years as Longshoreman. Is a
    citizen since 1906. Served in the Spanish-American War
    on Transport 22, "Massachusetts". Discharged on account
    of German Extraction.

Document 37c. Letter from John Gunlach to Honorable
W. B. Wilson, July 28, 1917. [National Archives]

International Longshoremens Ass'n
Local No. 306, Hoboken, N. J.

Affiliated with AMERICAN FEDERATION OF LABOR

PRESIDENT	SECRETARY
ADDRESS	ADDRESS

3.   *Hoboken, N. J.,* _____*191*

13.   AUGUST SCHWERDTFEGER: Working 6 years as Longshoreman. Has first paper three years. Drafted: No. 196. Discharged on account of German extraction.

14.   HINRICH KALLENDORF: Married; working 30 years as Longshoreman. Is a citizen since 1898. Discharged on account of German extraction.

15.   ROBERT BRASS: Married; working 25 years as Longshoreman. Is a citizen since 1902. Discharged on account of German extraction. Has a son liable to be drafted.

16.   FRITZ ROTHAUPT: Married; 3 children; working 13 years as Longshoreman. Is a citizen since 1915. Not permitted to work on account of German extraction.

17.   JAKOB WENDEL: Working 15 years as Longshoreman. Discharged on account of German extraction. No citizen.

18.   FRANZ YAAGE: Married; working 10 years as Longshoreman. Is a citizen since 1912. Not permitted to work on account of German extraction.

19.   HENRY HILKE: Married; working 17 years as Longshoreman. Is a citizen since 1912. Served in Spanish-American War on

International Longshoremens Ass'n
Local No. 306, Hoboken, N. J.

Affiliated with AMERICAN FEDERATION OF LABOR

PRESIDENT	SECRETARY
....	....
ADDRESS	**ADDRESS**
....	....

4.   *Hoboken, N. J.,* _____ *191*

Transport "City of Chester"& "Obdam".   Not permitted to

work on account of German extraction.

20.   ERNEST MÖNCH: Working 20 years as Longshoreman.   Not permitted

to work on account of German extraction.   No citizen.

21.   FREDERIK KLANG:: Married; working 28 years as Longshoreman.

Is a citizen since 1890.   One son is drafted: No. 1147.

Discharged on account of German extraction.

22.   FERDINAND GOLLIN: Married; working 21 years as Longshoreman.

Has son liable to be drafted.   Is a citizen since 1906.

Discharged on account of German extraction.

23.   ADAM FROMMER:: Married; working 18 years as Longshoreman.   Is

a citizen since 1905.   Served in Spanish-American War on

U. S. S. "Yale" as first-class fireman.   Discharged on ac-

count of German extraction.

24.   EMIL HORL: Married; working 6 years as Longshoreman.   Served

on Transport "Liona" during the Spanish-American War.

Took out first paper in 1900.   Not permitted to work on

account of German extraction.

25.   WILHELM BEHNKEN:: Working 30 years as Longshoreman.   Is a citi-

Document 37e. Letter from John Gunlach to Honorable
W. B. Wilson, July 28, 1917. [National Archives]

International Longshoremens Ass'n
Local No. 306, Hoboken, N. J.

Affiliated with AMERICAN FEDERATION OF LABOR

PRESIDENT	SECRETARY
ADDRESS	ADDRESS

5. *Hoboken, N. J.,* _____ *191*

zen since 1876. Discharged on account of German ex-

traction.

26. CHARLES SONDER: Working 4½ years as Longshoreman· No citi-

zen. Discharged on account of German extraction.

27. JOHANNES WILHELM ROPERS: Married; working 8 years as Long-

shoreman. Is a citizen since before April 2, 1917.

Discharged or not permitted to work on account of German

extraction.

28. WILLIAM SANKOWSKY: Married; working 27 years as Longshoreman,

and following up the sea on U. S. ships. Is a citizen sin

since 1906. Served on U. S. Transport 22 during Spanish-

American War. Not permitted to work on account of German

extraction.

29. MARTIN STICKERLING: Married; has 4 children; working 14 years

as Longshoreman. No citizen. Not permitted to work on

account of German extraction.

30. PETER STEINHOFER: Working 30 years as Longshoreman. Is citi-

zen since 1895. Served on U. S. Transport "Chester" dur-

ing Spanish-American War. Not permitted to work on ac-

count of German extraction.

Document 37f. Letter from John Gunlach to Honorable
W. B. Wilson, July 28, 1917. [National Archives]

International Longshoremens Ass'n
Local No. 306, Hoboken, N. J.

Affiliated with AMERICAN FEDERATION OF LABOR

PRESIDENT	SECRETARY
....	....
ADDRESS	ADDRESS
....	....

6.   *Hoboken, N. J.,*————————————*191*

51.   GUSTAVE SCHUSTER: Married: working 14th years as Longshoreman.
Is a citizen since 1914. Discharged on account of German
extraction.

52.   LORENZ HOCHSTRASSER: Married: has 3 children: working 9 years
as Longshoreman. Is a citizen since 1912. Discharged
on account of German extraction.

33.   HEINRICK BROCKMAN: Married; working 15 years as Longshoreman.
Is a citizen since 1898. Discharged on account of German
extraction.

34.   OTTO FREESE: Married; has 2 children; working 10 years as
Longshoreman. No citizen. Discharged on account of German
extraction.

35.   OTTO EGGERT: Married; has 3 children; working 16 years as
Longshoreman. No citizen. Not permitted to work on account of German extraction.

36.   WILHELM MOHLENBRING: Married; has 2 children; working 11 years
as Longshoreman. No citizen. Not permitted to work on
account of German extraction

37.   KLAUS HEITMAN: Working 15 years as Longshoreman. Has first

International Longshoremens Ass'n
Local No. 306, Hoboken, N. J.

Affiliated with AMERICAN FEDERATION OF LABOR

PRESIDENT	SECRETARY
ADDRESS	ADDRESS

7.   Hoboken, N. J.,——————————————191

papers 2½ years. Not permitted to work on account of

German extraction.

38.   ROBERT KLIEM: Married; working 16 years as Longshoreman. Is

citizen since 1912. Discharged on account of German extrac

tion.

39.   EWALD PETROSKY: Married; working 17 years as Longshoreman. No

citizen. Discharged on account of German extraction.

40.   CHARLES BAUMKIRCH: Married; working 18 years as Longshoreman.

One son drafted; one volunteered. Is citizen since 1908.

Not permitted to work on account of German extraction.

41.   FRITZ MEISNER: Married; has 3 children; working 5 years as

Longshoreman. One son liable to be drafted. Has receiv-

ed first paper 1 year. Not permitted to work on account

of German extraction.

42.   JOHN WOLF: Married; working 27 years as Longshoreman. Is a

citizen since 1900. Not permitted to work on account of

German extraction.

Document 37h. Letter from John Gunlach to Honorable
W. B. Wilson, July 28, 1917. [National Archives]

Document 38. Photograph, "Soldiers mustering out of Army," n.d.. [National Archives]

Document 39. Photograph, "Group of emigrants waiting for arrival of ship," Southhampton, England, n.d. [National Archives]

Document 40. Photograph, "Women's suffrage protestor with sign," November 19, 1918. [National Archives]

Document 41. Painting by Jacob Lawrence, "Negro Migration," n.d.
(National Archives Collection of Donated Materials). [National Archives]

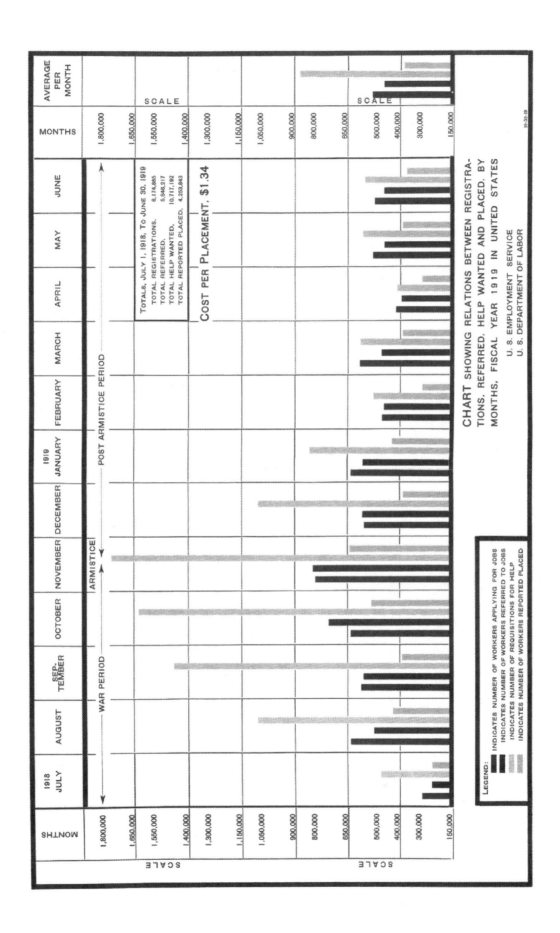

Document 42. U.S. Employment Service chart (July 1918-June 1919). [National Archives]

SIXTY-FOURTH CONGRESS.

JOHN T. WATKINS, LA., CHAIRMA
MARTIN A. MORRISON, IND.
ROBERT L. HENRY, TEX.
JAMES T. LLOYD, MO.
FRANK PARK, GA.
ROBERT CROSSER, OHIO.
JAMES H. MAYS, UTAH.
EDWARD B. ALMON, ALA.
MERRILL MOORES, IND.
WALTER W. MAGEE, N. Y.
ROBERT F. HOPWOOD, PA.
FRANK D. SCOTT, MICH.
WALTER R. STINESS, R. I.

LAMONT SEALS, CLERK.
W. K. WATKINS,
    REVISER OF THE STATUTES.

HOUSE OF REPRESENTATIVES U. S.

COMMITTEE ON

REVISION OF THE LAWS

WASHINGTON, D. C.

July 14, 1917.

Hon. W. B. Wilson,

    Secretary of Labor,

        Washington, D. C.

Mr. Secretary:

        During this time of War when it is
necessary to have laborers on the farm to produce
food and feed stuffs, there is an effort being
successfully carried out to have the colored labor
on the farms transported to the North to come in
competition with the white labor there.

        Agents are travelling about the South
making representations to the negroes which induce
them to leave the plantations in large numbers.

        The planters are becoming very much
exercised over it for fear that the depletion in
labor will prevent the crops from being harvested,
and considerable feeling is engendered. At Shreveport, Louisiana, in the Fourth Congressional District,
which I have the honor to represent, the negroes have
been leaving in bunches of twenty five to fifty every
Saturday night for the last three months. Last Monday
night about two hundred of them had congregated at

SIXTY-FOURTH CONGRESS.

JOHN T. WATKINS, LA., CHAIRMAN.
MARTIN A. MORRISON, IND.
ROBERT L. HENRY, TEX.
JAMES T. LLOYD, MO.
FRANK PARK, GA.
ROBERT CROSSER, OHIO.
JAMES H. MAYS, UTAH.
EDWARD B. ALMON, ALA.
MERRILL MOORES, IND.
WALTER W. MAGEE, N. Y.
ROBERT F. HOPWOOD, PA.
FRANK D. SCOTT, MICH.
WALTER R. STINESS, R. I.

LAMONT SEALS, CLERK.
W. K. WATKINS,
    REVISER OF THE STATUTES.

HOUSE OF REPRESENTATIVES U. S.
COMMITTEE ON
REVISION OF THE LAWS
WASHINGTON, D. C.

the Union Station to be carried over the Texas and Pacific Railroad on their way to Pittsburg, Pennsylvania, to work on the Pennsylvania Railroad.

These negroes were congregated under the instructions of F. R. Stier, a special agent of the Pennsylvania System, acting through Maurice Newman, a Labor Agent at Shreveport; but they were prevailed upon by the Sheriff of Caddo Parish and the Chief of Police of the city of Shreveport to return to their homes. It **is stated** that Mr. Stier said he was going to Galveston on a recruiting expedition. He is supposed to be the same person who had been collecting negro labor at Marshall, Texas, recently. I mention this particular incident to show what is happening in one locality in the South; but the movement is widespread and if there is any chance for it to be stopped through your instrumentality or any governmental regulations, I appeal to **you** in the strongest possible terms to take the matter in charge at as early a date as you can and put a stop to this traffic.

Of course you understand the demoralizing effect this movement will have in the North when these

Document 43b. Letter from J. T. Watkins to W. B. Wilson, July 14, 1917. [National Archives]

SIXTY-FOURTH CONGRESS.

JOHN T. WATKINS, LA., CHAIRMAN.
MARTIN A. MORRISON, IND.
ROBERT L. HENRY, TEX.
JAMES T. LLOYD, MO.
FRANK PARK, GA.
ROBERT CROSSER, OHIO.
JAMES H. MAYS, UTAH.
EDWARD B. ALMON, ALA.
MERRILL MOORES, IND.
WALTER W. MAGEE, N. Y.
ROBERT F. HOPWOOD, PA.
FRANK D. SCOTT, MICH.
WALTER R. STINESS, R. I.

LAMONT SEALS, CLERK.
W. K. WATKINS,
REVISER OF THE STATUTES.

HOUSE OF REPRESENTATIVES U. S.

COMMITTEE ON
REVISION OF THE LAWS

WASHINGTON, D. C.

negroes come in competition with the white labor there,

as this was demonstrated at East Saint Louis, Illinois.

I am, with greatest respect,

Yours truly,

J. T. Watkins,

M. C. Fourth La. Dist.

Document 43c. Letter from J. T. Watkins to W. B. Wilson, July 14, 1917. [National Archives]

March 18, 1921.

M e m o r a n d u m :

    From: The Director of Negro Economics
      To: T h e   A s s i s t a n t   S e c r e t a r y
    Subject: Functions and work of Negro Economics Advisory Service.

I. Underlying Facts of the Work:

There are four cardinal facts which have been given due consideration in the development of this work:

1. The two races are thrown together in their daily
work, the majority of the employers and a large number
of the employees having relations with Negro employees
being white persons.   These conditions give rise to
misunderstandings, prejudices, antagonisms, fears, and
suspicions.   These facts must be recognized and dealt
with in a statesmanlike manner.
2. The problems are local in character, arising,
as they do, between local employers and local employees.
The people, however, in local communities, need the
vision of national policies, plans, and standards to
apply to their local situations.
3. Any plan or program should be based upon the
desire and need of cooperation between white employers
and representatives of Negro wage earners, and, wherever possible, white wage earners.
4. Negroes constitute about one tenth of the total
population of the United States and about one seventh
of the working population gainfully employed.   They
have been migrating increasingly in large numbers from
the rural districts to urban centers and from the South
to the North for more than forty years.
    Therefore, it is reasonable and right that they
be accorded representation from their ranks, in counsel,
when matters affecting them are being considered and
decided.

These facts being true it is evident that the adjustment of mil-
lions of uneducated wage earners from rural regions to town life and
from agricultural work to industrial work, as well as the readjustments

in agricultural regions due to the increasing migration from the rural districts to the urban centers during the past fifty years is a tremendous task, even without the serious racial and sectional complications that have arisen.

The efforts of the Department of Labor, therefore, in dealing with the relations of Negro workers, white workers, and employers widely affect the economic interests of the entire Nation and are of vital concern to employers, white workers, and the public-at-large no less than to Negro wage-earners. Cooperation, mutual understanding, goodwill and tolerance are the best and only principles that will promote the interests of all concerned.

II. Some Problems of Negro Labor:

Practically every question which arises, like that connected with the coal miners, the steel workers and the meat-packing employees, involves considerable numbers of Negro workers and raises problems of their relations to white workers and employers. In addition there are some special problems more directly related to the internal affairs of Negroes and their relations to employers. Among them are the following:

1. The thousands of Negro workers in war industries who had to be shifted back to post-war industries along with the other workers call for special attention similar to the period when they were being shifted into war industries.

2. Probably between 400,000 and 500,000 workers migrated from the South to northern industries. The difficulties of cooperative adjustment of white wage earners and Negro wage earners in the industrial communities where they must find community life in contact with each other were increased.

3. Special problems connected with the entrance of colored women into industry and special problems in domestic and personal service arise from time to time.

4. The problems of improving the conditions, increasing the efficiency, and encouraging the thrift of Negro workers were probably greater during the war and still remain as reconstruction problems.

5. In the South the common interests of white employers who want to engage the services which the Negro wage earner has to offer and the desire of the worker for wages in return make the adjustment of the Negro labor situation one of the most far-reaching factors in bringing about just and amicable race relations. The migration and war restlessness of the two races creates problems which the labor nexus may be very effective in settling.

Document 44b. Memorandum from the Director of Negro Economics
Division to the Asst. Secretary of Labor, March 18, 1921. [National Archives]

6. The adjustment of farm tenantry and of the labor situation in the South is very largely a problem of Negro labor.

7. The improvement of living and working conditions, including such questions as housing, sanitation, and recreation of Negro wage earners, should receive more attention during this period of reconstruction and peace time than they did before or during the Great War period.

III. Functions of the Work:

In the development of this work of the Negro Economics Service its staff has been called upon to advise and inform the Secretary and the several chiefs and employees of the bureaus and divisions of the Department in all matters, such as policies, plans, personnel, etc., affecting Negroes and their relations with white workers and employers. The Secretary also approved the policy of furnishing advice and information to individuals, employers, and organizations, to the end that cooperation, mutual understanding and goodwill might be promoted through such mediation and conciliation.

The Secretary defined the functions of this service in the following words:

"Staff employees dealing with Negro wage-earners, although not being removed from the authority and instructions of chiefs of divisions to which they are rendering service, act under the general supervision and authority of the Director of Negro Economics, with the agreeable understanding and approval of the chiefs of their respective divisions;"

and that

"It be clearly understood that there is no desire or intention to establish a dual direction of the staff employees dealing with Negro wage-earners;"

but that

"The purpose is to secure the advice of the Director of Negro Economics before any work dealing with Negro wage-earners is undertaken, and to keep him advised of the progress of such work so that the Department may have the benefit of his judgment in all matters affecting Negroes."

The Director of Negro Economics is under the personal supervision of the Secretary and does not have departmental executive authority.

In carrying out these functions it developed that the Director of Negro Economics needed assistants and field agents through whom he might gather and furnish information and advice, and might keep in touch with the local fields for purposes of mediation and conciliation. This field service has been furnished in two ways:

1. Staff employees of divisions or bureaus, with the consent and under the direction of their respective chiefs, have cooperated in furnishing service to the Director of Negro Economics.
2. Special agents or employees have been detailed to the Secretary's office for service under the immediate supervision of the Director of Negro Economics.

IV. Field Organization:

The field organization has suffered severely in the past eighteen months because there have been no funds available for the necessary staff employees to keep in touch with local fields. The following, however, is the plan as successfully carried out during about the first eighteen months of the work, some parts of which plan are still operating as far as touch can be kept with the local fields by correspondence of limited character with reliable persons.

1. Negro Workers' Advisory Committees, composed of representatives of the white employers, Negro workers, and, wherever possible, white workers, were formed during the War, in eleven states. County committees and city committees were appointed by the Department of Labor under state committees, with local endorsements. Most of the personnel of such committees had the sanction of local governmental officials. These committees were formed after the holding of joint conferences of white and colored representatives, which conferences were called either by the Governors of the states or with the consent and cooperation of the Governors, the Councils of National Defense, or other official or semi-official local authorities. Here and there some of these committees have taken on local connections or have been reorganized under local leadership and without further connection with this Department.

Through these committees, however, we have listed more than 1,000 able and responsible white and colored citizens in the most strategic labor centers in these eleven states, and through them, as correspondents, we have from time to time kept informed, as far as volunteer and informal correspondence can do, of the local labor conditions.

Document 44d. Memorandum from the Director of Negro Economics Division to the Asst. Secretary of Labor, March 18, 1921. [National Archives]

U. S. DEPARTMENT OF LABOR
U.S. Employment Service
With the Co-operation of the Council of National Defense.

December 5, 1918.

BUREAUS FOR RETURNING SOLDIERS AND SAILORS.

1.   GENERAL DESCRIPTION.

  1.   Purpose.

       To establish in every community, from the small town to the largest
city, a bureau where the returning soldier or sailor may ascertain what employment is open for him.   Many soldiers are returning home; many are going to
cities where they are relatively unknown.   Wherever they go; it is the duty
of the community to see that every possible opportunity is given to them to
get jobs - to get the best jobs for which they are qualified.   These men gave
up their work at the country's call, without hesitation.   To some of them,
their old positions remain open; with others, such is not the case.   Still
others have acquired new purpose and strength and in many cases new skill,
which fits them for better work than they had formerly.   It is both a national
and a community duty to see that as they come back everything is done to enable
them to return to their livelihood in the positions where they can do most
effective work.

  2.   Agencies Concerned in Meeting Problem.

       In every community there are many bodies, such as churches, lodges,
and local branches of national women's organizations, and such bodies as the
Red Cross, Y.M.C.A., National Catholic War Council, Jewish Welfare Board,
Salvation Army, American Federation of Labor, the War Camp Community Service,
draft boards, and others, which are preparing to find employment for the
returning soldiers and sailors.   Unless coordinated, the work of these
organizations will overlap, with corresponding loss in efficiency.   No one
of them alone will be able to get more than partial information as to the
available opportunities in the cities and very few will be in touch with
possibilities in other communities.
       The U. S. Employment Service is the official Governmental organiza-
tion charged with the duty of helping secure positions for returning soldiers
and sailors, as well as war workers and others.   It has Community Labor Boards
composed of one representative of employers, one representative of labor, and
one representative of the Service, throughout the country, over 1580 in number.
It also has some 850 offices scattered throughout the country and has volunteer
agents in other places.
       With the approval of the Secretaries of War, Navy, Agriculture,
Interior, Commerce and Labor, sitting together as a Council of National Defense,
the U. S. Employment Service, with the assistance of the State Councils of
Defense and their Community Councils, has undertaken to organize in every city
and town throughout the country a Bureau for Returning Soldiers and Sailors.
The joint telegram of instructions sent by the Employment Service and Council
of National Defense to their respective State organizations is appended hereto
and constitutes the fundamental basis of the plan thus officially adopted.
The full cooperation of the appended list of national organizations is assured.

1.

3.   General Method of Operation.

The returning soldier or sailor may call personally at the Bureau, but frequently will call upon some one of the cooperating agencies. It is not necessary that applications for work by these men should be made at any one particular place.

It is, however, necessary that so far as possible all information as to positions open should be centered in one office and there kept strictly up to date. Such information will thus be a common pool on which all co-operating agencies will be able to draw. Co-operating agencies will register at this central office all opportunities for employment which come to their attention. Employers should be urged as a patriotic duty to register their opportunities for employment at the Central Bureau, with specifications as to types and kinds of men wanted and other necessary details. They should keep the Bureau informed as such positions are filled or as new jobs are open. The full resources of the Bureau will be open without charge to any returning soldier or sailor, regardless of where he first makes application. The Bureau should use all means at its disposal to furnish returning soldiers and sailors with correct information on the various questions that will confront them, or direct them to places where such information can be obtained.

4.   Returning War Workers.

While designed primarily for soldiers and sailors, in many communities the Bureau will care also for those civilians who have left their peace time jobs to take positions with concerns engaged in doing war work. In many places the facilities of the Employment Service are sufficient in themselves to care for the civilian workers; in other places it may become a community necessity that the Central Bureau should be for Soldiers and Sailors and War Workers so as to give assistance to civilians who have been engaged in war work and who cannot find employment.

2.

"Carry On"

OFFICIAL PUBLICATION OF THE WOMAN'S COMMITTEE (MICHIGAN DIVISION)
COUNCIL OF NATIONAL DEFENSE

No. 2   Kalamazoo, Michigan, Dec. 21, 1918

DR. ANNA HOWARD SHAW WRITES MESSAGE TO WOMEN OF AMERICA

Outlining the post-war activities which become the duties of the women of America, Dr. Anna Howard Shaw, vice chairman of the field division of the Council of National Defense, has issued from Washington a ringing call to American women in the following message:

TO THE WOMEN OF AMERICA:

The victory for which America has organized and labored, sacrificed and borne is about to be ours. Although a period of months must elapse before the declaration of peace, the enemy is vanquished and we may look forward to the end of the great war as imminent.

Toward the accomplishment of this victory, the women of America have contributed their part. Whether we were asked to save food, to enter industry in the places men had hitherto filled, to make bandages for the wounded, to sell and buy bonds, to give up husbands, brothers and sons to the danger of death or to cross the harzardous seas and stand beside them as nurses, we have responded by the thousands or hundred thousands as the call demanded.

We have done more. We have organized a great second army of defense to preserve the home, to care for the children, to protect women from the dangers of industry, with the avowed purpose of making the country for which our men have died worthy of their sacrifice. With this in mind, we taught thrift and economy to our people, we planned and carried out a program for children's year, we advocated proper standards for women in industry, we worked on health and educational problems.

This task is not finished with the imminence of victory, not even with victory itself. There remains the greater and more difficult part: To garner the fruits of victory. It is not enough for women who have given up their sons on the battlefield, that Alsace-Lorraine shall be given back to France; there must be given to our sons, or other mothers' sons, a chance to grow up well and strong here in America. It is not enough for widowed mothers, that autocracy across the sea is dead; there must be freedom here at home for their daughters to win their daily bread under conditions that make for health and happiness and honor. The work of the women of America will not be done until the fruits of victory shall include the making of America a better, safer place for all the children than it was before August, 1914.

This is not reconstruction; it is not even readjustment. There must be a measure of both and both include problems in which women and their interests are a serious factor and in the solution of which they must have a voice. This is an intention that our sacrifices shall not have been in vain. It is a realization of the aim for which we made them.

In war time, it was found that what had been called "woman's interests," namely, food, thrift, health, morals, were the interests of a whole people and had an integral part in the organization for victory. It was also found that they were intimately tied up with the great financial, industrial programs. In peace times, they will no less be the interests of the whole nation, and in the realization of war aims, they have an important place. No peace that ignores them, no program that overlooks them, can claim to represent the aims for which we fought. It is therefore becomes the duty of the womanhood of America to interest itself vitally in the terms of the peace and to prepare ourselves to perform our obligation to make victory complete.

During the movement of a nation from a war basis to a peace basis, great changes must inevitably take place, changes economic, industrial, social. No thinking person can expect that the change will be altogether back to a pre-war basis. The women can be no more relieved from their obligation to see that these changes make a richer heritage, healthier environment and freer opportunity for their children than they were from their obligation, now faithfully performed, to see that their soldier sons had every protection, physical and moral, thrown about them, both in the camp and on the firing line. They cannot neglect their duty to the sons and daughters of the men who will not come back to them nor can they meet the returning soldiers with anything less than an honest, "We have done all we promised you."

For all these reasons it is imperative that there shall be no demobilization of the woman power of America. It must remain organized, equipped and ready for action. We do not know the full program that will be laid before us; we cannot say precisely what our part in it will be. But we know it will include those things that women have ever held dear: The safeguarding of little children, the education of youth, the health of a people, and such great tasks as supplying to every willing worker, a job, and providing for the whole world, food. What we do know is: There can be no great performance in which women do not play a part.

Our present duty, then, is to emulate our brothers and sons in France. here the men wait with vigilance as keen as ever, ready to spring to action at the word of command, whether that word be to attack the enemy again, or to garrison a vanquished foe. We, no more than they, are mustered out.

—ANNA HOWARD SHAW.

Document 46. Dr. Anna Howard Shaw's article from Carry On (publication of Council of National Defense), December 21, 1918. [National Archives]

Gee A Kennedy
1418 Hancock Ave W.
Detroit. Mich.

Honorable James J.Davis,
Secretary of Labor,
Washington, D.C.

My Dear Mr Davis,

     As a citizen of Detroit,interested very much in the main features of your splendid address delivered at Belle Isle Park on Labor Day permit me to congratulate you on the clear and forceable manner in which your views were presented. Of late,I have been giving some study to the immigration question---the character of the immigrant coming to America, especially during the last decade and I listened with a keen interest to what you had to say on this topic in your address.

     During the late war,I made a number of "4 minute talks" which touched very briefly on the question and before audiences which had quite a per-centage of recent arrivals from eastern and southern Europe,where illiteracy and decadent morals are evidently good passports for American emmigration and future American citizenship. The mines and lumber district of northern Minnesota,where the slacker and the bolshevist was a common source of trouble,was my territory and it took tact and a proper sense of the situation sometimes to get a respectful hearing. But I secured this hearing,because of the presence in every gathering of this sort of a large number of real Americans who usually dominate as leaders and on whose shoulders will always rest the responsibility of molding and directing this foreign material into some semblance of American citizenship. The process in some cases is a slow one,often is an utter failure and making it clear to the minds of those who gave up their time to a close study of the question,that our so called "melting pot" is only a myth---the dream of the alchemist to convert the baser metals into the gold of racial values and real Americans.

As Secretary of Labor, you have a very heavy burden on your shoulders when you have to deal with this question, for it is involved in many of our economic troubles and the man who will help to solve, or clear up a few things connected with it during his administration, should have the cordial support of every true American.

If America in the past has been an asylum for the oppressed and a land of opportunity, it has also been a rendezvous for the criminal and the degenerate, and no city in America knows this better than the city of Detroit. Its jails, house of correction, orphanages and feeble minded institutes are crowded to the doors, and the cause can be traced very largely to one source--illadvised administration of our immigration problem. Any legislation that you can suggest which will correct the faults of the past, will not only distinguish your administration for accomplishing this, but it may be the turning point for better things in the future of American citizenship.

I am enclosing a clipping from the Detroit Free Press, in which I called attention to the bearing the race question has on this immigration problem and I feel that I am not alone in thinking that it is very serious phase of it. I would be glad to offer any service in my power to bring about a change for the better, if it were possible to organize a program for practical education on the subject in every state of the Union.

Lacking this, you have my best wishes for the success of your Administration .

Very cordially yours,

Geo A Kennedy

Teaching With Documents Order Form

World War I: The Home Front

You may order copies of the following document in its original size:

Document	Price	Qty.	Total
Document 42. *(11x17, color)* U.S. Employment Service chart (July 1918-June 1919).	$14.00		
Add 5% MD Sales Tax (if applicable)			
Shipping & Handling (Ground Shipping: $10.00, Air Shipping: $22.00)			
Total			

Billing Address:

_____

_____

_____

_____

Shipping Address: (if different from Billing Address)

_____

_____

_____

_____

☐ Check Enclosed payable to Graphic Visions Associates

☐ VISA   ☐ Mastercard   ☐ American Express

_____/_____/_____/_____/   _____/_____/   _____

Credit Card Number   Exp. Date   Authorized Signature

(_____)_____   (_____)_____

Telephone   Fax

Mail Order To: Graphic Visions
640 East Diamond Avenue, Ste. F
Gaithersburg, MD 20877